ANCIENT HERBS

P9-APN-703

ANCIENT HERBS
In the J. Paul Getty Museum Gardens

Jeanne D'Andrea

Illustrations by
Martha Breen Bredemeyer

The J. Paul Getty Museum, Malibu, California

© 1982 The J. Paul Getty Museum
17985 Pacific Coast Highway
Malibu, California 90265-5799

Library of Congress catalogue number 82-81306

ISBN number 0-89236-035-6

Designed by Alexander Pearman
Type set in Baskerville by Characters & Color
Printing by Alan Lithograph, Inc., Los Angeles
Binding by Roswell Bindery, Phoenix

Second printing 1989

Cover: *Rosa canina* Linnaeus; *R. X. damascena; R. gallica 'Officinalis.' Rosaceae.* (See p. 70.)

CONTENTS

ACKNOWLEDGMENTS

*H*erbs in antiquity touch on so many aspects of human activity that the advice of classicists, botanists, horticulturalists, linguists, medical historians, physicians, and sociologists has been essential. The first Getty Museum publication on the subject was *The Herb in Antiquity* written in 1976 by Deborah Ashin in response to the interest of visitors. My great appreciation and gratitude go to John MacGregor IV of the Huntington Library Botanical Gardens for his numerous suggestions based on a deep understanding of both plants and antiquity; he and James A. Bauml were unsparingly generous. Equally so were Kenneth Donahue, Professor Daniel Glaser, Pearl Glaser, and Jeanne Morgan, each of whom I thank for careful, perceptive readings of the manuscript and valuable critical suggestions. I am grateful to Professor Wilhelmina Jashemski, whose comments were received with appreciative interest, as were those of Stephen Spurr. I should also like to thank Professors Phyllis Pray Bober and Jerry Stannard; the physicians Francis M. Crage and Edward Shapiro; and Frances Crage, Carolyn Dzur, and Emmett R. Wemple for their assistance with specific problems. The intricacies of finding correct Greek equivalents for the English herb names were untangled by Professor David Blank and Katherine Kiefer.

In addition to Director Stephen Garrett of the J. Paul Getty Museum, I should especially like to thank Curator Jirí Frel and Faya Causey Frel. Sandra Knudsen Morgan, Head of Publications, offered constantly thoughtful and pertinent critical assistance. Volunteer Nini Lyddy assisted in initial preparations for this edition. Richard Naranjo, Chief Gardener, has supported the project with personal interest, enthusiasm, and a growing garden.

The effectiveness of this edition depends very much on the visual contributions of Martha Breen Bredemeyer, whose illustrations have delighted all of us, and of Alexander Pearman, whose graphic design has been so sensitive to the subject. Both have been responsive colleagues, as has Elizabeth Jane Foster who typed, read, and proofread the manuscript at every turn. My thanks to each of them and to all those who have shared their libraries and ideas about herbs in antiquity.

Note to the second printing (1989)
The Museum staff has undergone many changes since the first printing in 1982, including changes of name and title for some of the contributors to this volume. The Museum remains grateful to each of them for their contributions to what has become a very successful publication, and we therefore reprint the original acknowledgments in full.

PREFACE

*T*ender and fragrant, acrid and indestructible, the parsley and onions we use every day were also used daily by the Greeks and the Romans. Our senses can respond to the past directly, not only through art but also through herbs. The same basil, garlic, rosemary, and thyme that grew two thousand years ago at the Villa dei Papiri in Herculaneum can be seen and smelled, touched and tasted in the evocative herb garden of the J. Paul Getty Museum.

In ancient Greece and Rome herbs were eaten, imbibed, and applied to wounds. Olive, laurel, parsley, and pine were bound into wreaths to crown the winners of the Greek games. Fragrant herbs honored the gods, embalmed the dead, and purified disease-ridden rooms. Hundreds of medicinal herbs were used and catalogued by Greek and Roman physicians. Fresh herbs for all these purposes could be gathered wild in the countryside, bought at local markets, or grown at home in kitchen gardens.

Herbs in the ancient world are closely linked to the prowess of the Greek and Roman gods, the whims and wisdom of emperors, and the innovations of physicians and philosophers. Prometheus carried the gift of fire in a hollow fennel stalk, Nero kicked Poppaea to death and then used a year's supply of Rome's cinnamon to bury her, and Hippocrates stressed herbal cures when he drafted the ground rules for modern medicine. Our primary sources of information are the works of ancient artists, authors, and scientists— as well as the mounting archaeological evidence. From the first literary masterpieces of the western world, Homer's *Iliad* and *Odyssey,* to the extravagant pretensions of the Roman empire brilliantly parodied by Petronius in the *Satyricon,* pungent, aromatic herbs appear. The Greeks and Romans were the heirs of a tradition that had already begun some 160,000 years before, the approximate age of interglacial human deposits in which the common herb oregano, or wild marjoram, has been found.

Within the ancient myths and folklore about sacred or potent plants lies some very durable knowledge. Today, herbs and plants continue to have innumerable industrial uses in addition to their uses in food, clothing, and medicine. The structure of modern pharmacopoeia itself is patterned on our historical knowledge of these plants. While most of today's medicines are chemical-pharmaceutical equivalents of age-old remedies, recent research in medical and industrial applications of the plants themselves—the botanicals or galenicals—has led to dramatic new plant-derived drugs such as vinblastine and vincristine for the treatment of cancer.

An herb is usually defined as a plant that dies back to the ground after flowering. Unlike trees or shrubs, most herbs develop no permanent woody structure. τò φοτόν and *herba* to most ancient Greeks and Romans had a broader meaning that included almost all plants and grasses. In non-scientific usage, all plants valued for their magical, medicinal, aromatic, and flavoring characteristics, or for their coloring matter, traditionally have been considered herbs.

This book explores some of the herbal beliefs and practices of the ancient Greeks and Romans that probably influenced the occupants of the Villa dei Papiri whose splendid house and garden are recreated in Malibu.

Flora/Core, after a fresco from Stabiae, ca. 50 B.C. Naples, Museo Nazionale.

THE J. PAUL GETTY MUSEUM HERB GARDEN

*A*ncient painting and literature, and modern archaeology, tell us of the value of gardens in antiquity. A wealthy family during Roman times might have a house with gardens within the city of Rome or its suburbs as well as several country villas. In smaller towns, even modest citizens and tradespeople had small gardens that seemed to combine utility with pleasure or relaxation. Often landscapes and garden scenes were painted on garden walls to make smaller gardens seem larger, greener, and more appealing. People without gardens could sometimes enjoy them, as they do today, through a window that looked out on an adjacent garden or orchard.

Villas near Pompeii and Herculaneum, as elsewhere in ancient Italy, were often vast country estates. Outside the city wealthy Romans deliberately oriented their buildings to vast perspectives of the same scenery that artists painted on the walls of their town houses. Elaborate villas in Campania were often built on breathtaking sites, capturing views of both the mountains and the Mediterranean. Natural scenery, formal gardens, walks, colonnades, kitchen gardens, and the buildings themselves were all integrated with the landscape in a time when social and economic life was closely tied to the richness of the land.

The Villa dei Papiri just outside the walls of Herculaneum, which the J. Paul Getty Museum building recreates, reflects a change that occurred in architecture and attitude in the second century B.C. At that time the wealthy Samnites who had conquered Campania several centuries earlier began to build grander houses than before, influenced by the contemporary Hellenistic style of Greece. As the Italic houses became larger and more elegant, the peristyle was also added—a courtyard that in Greek buildings was not treated as a garden. In Italy the peristyle became a garden court, often planted with large trees and a few shrubs, a garden that was easy to maintain.

Water was not readily available in the Hellenistic cities, and since a year-round garden was desirable, its planting was essentially evergreen: laurel, rosemary, myrtle, oleander, acanthus, box, vine, and ivy. After the Roman aqueducts of the first centuries B.C. and A.D. brought water to houses with far greater ease, allowing pools, fountains, and low formal planting, many gardens took on quite a new aspect. Among the green plants, flowers were mingled in their seasons, grown not only for color in the garden but also for their blossoms to be woven into garlands for the household gods and festive occasions, and for their petals, leaves, seeds, and roots to be used as medicine or food. Recent excavations by Dr. Jashemski have revealed that most of the precious aqueduct water for Pompeii's houses seems to have been piped into the gardens, an eloquent testimony to their importance. Sculpture, too, found its way into the garden during this period, making its unique contribution to the garden's changing appearance. At the Villa dei Papiri, ninety marbles and bronzes (today in the Naples Museum) have been excavated. Many of them are garden sculptures, such as the famous *Resting Hermes* and *Sleeping Faun.* Replicas of many fill the corners and colonnades of the Getty Museum's gardens.

When lava and ash from Vesuvius engulfed Pompeii and Herculaneum in A.D. 79, sealing off the town from those inhabitants lucky enough to have survived, it also sealed off rich evidence of the life and world of ancient Rome. Although plant material is less tangible than other physical remains, archaeologists and botanists have found ways to identify some of these plants by studying root cavities, pollen, and carbonized remains—such as the carbonized laurel branch found in the *lapilli* in the large peristyle garden of the House of the Faun in Pompeii. Ancient reliefs, sculpture, and paintings of plants on garden walls are also important primary sources.

Excavations of the Villa dei Papiri, carried out under the patronage of the Bourbon kings of Naples in the eighteenth century, did not progress as far as the living quarters of the house nor to many of the outlying areas of the enormous villa. As further excavations have not yet been possible because of the dangerous underground volcanic gases, there is no specific information about either the existence or the design of an agricultural garden on the villa, although evidence shows that such gardens were clearly essential to villa life.

The Getty Museum Herb Garden (see foldout map at end of book) is located outside the west wall of the main peristyle garden, accessible through entrances at either end of the portico. Since the peristyle itself is as large as a town forum, the herb garden that runs its length has spacious planting beds and paths. Designed by Dennis Kurutz of Emmett L. Wemple & Associates, the herb garden occupies an area that in the original villa seems to have been an exercise track later converted to a garden area with walkways around a pool and a fountain. Geometric beds of low-lying herbs fan out from a central well planted with ivy and flowers. Height is achieved with taller plants and with apple, fig, and citrus trees. Opposite the peristyle wall, the garden is flanked by terraced olives, cypresses, and fruit trees, a terrain similar to that of the original villa. Paths among the herb beds allow strolling and gardening access. An extended perspective through the garden leads to a pergola at the far end, and the sea beyond completes the vista.

Similarities of climate between southern Italy and southern California allow the same herbs to grow in the recreated gardens as were grown in ancient Campania and in other parts of the ancient Mediterranean world. Among the herbs cultivated by the ancient Greeks and Romans are twenty-one that were highly favored and continuously used for ritual, medicine, and food. All these herbs are grown today in the museum herb garden, including basil, garlic, mint, oregano, parsley, and thyme. Some of these herbs such as the laurel trees, the rosemary and myrtle hedges, and the roses of the main peristyle garden, also appear in the more formal gardens of the museum, as they would have in an ancient villa.

The herbs are most beautiful in May, when many of them are tender and fragrant and delicately blooming in a garden similar to one in daily use near Herculaneum two thousand years ago.

His own sandals
he immediately threw off
on the sea-shore.
Then he wove
a new pair,
indescribable,
unimaginable, they were
marvelous creations:
tamerisks twisted together
with myrtle branches.
After he tied together
an armful of this wood,
he tied these quick sandals
to his feet, gently,
with their leaves.
Then the glorious Argeiphontes
left Pieria,
avoiding a wearisome trip
by wearing such original shoes,
and hurrying, like a man set for a long trip.

Then he gathered up
a lot of wood,
and tried to figure out
the art of fire:
he took a laurel branch
and struck it up and down
on a pomegranate stick
in his other hand.
It breathed warm smoke.
So it was Hermes
who was the first
to come up with fire,
and the way to make it.
In an underground trench
he put all kinds
of flammable material.
The flame lit
and sent far off
a great blast of blazing fire.

* * * *

From: The Hymn to Hermes,
The Homeric Hymns

Victory hanging a shield on a laurel tree: VICTORIA AUGUSTI, bronze sestertius of the emperor Vitellius, A.D. 69.

THE HERBS OF THE GODS

*H*erbs had a potent value for the ancient Greeks and Romans. Not only were they used to alleviate illness and enhance food, as they still are today, but they were sources of power over the environment. They were intimately associated with ritual, magic, and especially religion, all of which controlled and shaped the lives of the Greeks and the Romans much as science and engineering shape ours today. The religions of these two ancient Mediterranean cultures are expressed in the Greek myths and the Roman rituals.

Man's myths are his views of himself and his world. When Homer's *Iliad* and *Odyssey* appeared early in the first millennium B.C., Greek mythology and religion already had evolved from an intricate blend of pre-Greek, Egyptian, and Asiatic beliefs. The majestic Homeric poems offer the first clear images of the classical gods, radiant deities understood by all Greeks. These gods were seen as immortals in human form. Endowed with human appetites and passions, they governed the world of nature and men. Powerful, swift, clever, and wise, the gods were often described as sweet-smelling, exuding the scents of herbs and flowers as they moved in fragrant halls and meadows.

Zeus, the sky god, controlled the quarrelsome Olympians with his thunderbolts, while other gods ruled the plant and animal worlds. Apollo, the god of light and truth who killed as well as cured, first taught men the art of healing through his son Asclepius, the god of medicine. Artemis was the goddess of all wild things and Hestia the goddess of house and hearth. The Greek traveler and geographer Pausanias comments in the second century A.D. that a horde of totem beasts, birds, and plants was offered annually to Artemis. At the temple of Apollo in Delphi the oracle was attended by a priest who interpreted her frenzied utterances induced perhaps by chewing bay leaves, Apollo's sacred plant. The rose of the goddess Aphrodite was said to have sprung from the blood of her lover Adonis. Also sacred to Aphrodite was the myrtle, shared with the endlessly inventive Hermes.

Not long after Homer, two extended poems appeared that are usually credited to Hesiod, a poet-farmer from Boeotia. Although Homer and Hesiod agreed on the *personae* of the Olympian gods, Homer's stories are of human gods and heroic men, while Hesiod's *Theogony* outlines the creation of the universe and the genealogy of the gods. Hesiod details the exchange between the wily Prometheus and the angry Zeus, in which Prometheus steals the "far-seen gleam of unwearying fire" in a hollow fennel stalk and thus gives fire to men. Today, in parts of rural Greece, burning charcoal is still carried in giant fennel stalks. (Giant fennel, *Ferula communis,* is classified in a genus distinct from garden fennel, *Foeniculum vulgare,* see page 46.)

How close the Greek gods were to the productivity of the earth is shown clearly in Hesiod's second poem, *The Works and Days.* Addressed to his conniving brother who was to share their inherited farm, it is a compendium of admonitions and counsels as well as a document of life on the land. Hesiod tells his brother how to address the gods, his neighbors, and his farm help; when to dig the vineyards; when to marry and whom;

what is practical winter clothing; how to make a plough-beam (poles of laurel or elm are least likely to be worm-eaten, but the share should be oak, the beam holm oak); how to read the seasons from the cry of the crane; to wake early and to work long. On spring planting he advises him to pray and then to sow carefully:

> Make your prayers to Zeus of the ground
> and holy Demeter
> that the sacred yield of Demeter may grow complete,
> and be heavy.
> Do this when you begin your first planting, when
> gripping the handle
> in one hand, you come down hard with the goad
> on the back of your oxen
> as they lean into the pin of the straps.
> Have a small boy helping you
> by following and making it hard for the birds
> with a mattock
> covering the seed over. It is best to do things
> systematically,
> since we are only human, and disorder
> is our worst enemy.

Demeter and Dionysus were the two regenerative gods of the earth and the underworld who were most intimately linked to the cycle of plant growth that sustained human life. In the Homeric hymns, written by unknown poets in the style of Homer after Hesiod's time, Demeter is the sorrowing goddess who gives rich harvests and then each winter makes the earth barren. The myth of Demeter expresses the cycle of nature as the loss of the goddess' daughter Core, later called Persephone. Hades had fallen in love with Core, but his brother Zeus found it awkward to consent to a marriage (Zeus, Hades, and Demeter were siblings, and Core and Iacchus were children of Demeter and Zeus). Hades abducted Core as she "was gathering flowers—roses, and crocuses, and fair violets, in the soft meadow, and lilies, and hyacinths, and the narcissus which the earth brought forth as a snare to the fair-haired maiden." Demeter veiled herself and wandered in search of Core for nine days and nights, at last learning from the Sun of the abduction. On the tenth day she came to Eleusis, to the palace of King Celeus and his wife Metaneira. Refusing wine, Demeter requested barley-water flavored with mint (a precedent for the draught given the initiates of her cult). After consenting to be wet nurse to the newborn prince, she began to transform him into a god by placing him in the fire at night. When his frightened mother cried out, the goddess revealed herself and commanded that a temple for her worship be built at Eleusis. Installed there, she vowed the earth would stay barren until her daughter was returned. One by one the other gods pleaded with Demeter to relent. When she still refused, Zeus persuaded Hades to return Persephone to her mother; but Hades first fed her sweet pomegranate seeds (a symbol of death) to ensure her return. At last Zeus ordered a compromise: Persephone would spend a third of each year with Hades in the underworld and the rest of the year with her mother and the other gods.

Men prayed to Demeter in the fields and on the threshing floors. Her chief celebration at harvest time was a simple feast that later became the worship called the Eleusinian mysteries, observed for many centuries at the great temple of Eleusis near Athens. Little is known of the secret rites except that the initiate at first was shrouded in darkness, and after a nine-day fast was given a draught of *kykeon*—the barley-water mixed with fresh mint mentioned in the Homeric hymn to Demeter, and the common beverage of workers in the field.

Symbols of love, the myrtle tree and the rose were sacred to the goddess Aphrodite, and from the time of Homer they appear often in Greek literature. The soldier-poet Archilochus, born on the Cycladic island of Paros, is credited with inventing iambic verse. Admired in antiquity as both a lyric poet and a satirist, he was described by Meleager as "a thistle with graceful leaves." We know of his passionate response to Greek life in the seventh century B.C. from fragments of his marching songs, his elegies, and his fragile love lyrics. In one vivid fragment Archilochus tenderly observes a girl:

> She held
>   a sprig of myrtle she'd picked
> And a rose
> That pleased her most
> Of those on the bush
> And her long hair shaded
>   her shoulders and back.

Dionysus, like the goddess Demeter, personified fertility. An immigrant god from Thrace in the early first millennium B.C., he was according to myth a child of Zeus by the Theban princess Semele. Most often he is represented wreathed in vine leaves and holding aloft grape clusters, as the reveling and triumphant god of the vine, inspiring his first followers—the satyrs and maenads—to a frenzied dance, swinging staffs and torches and devouring wild animals. Milder festivals were celebrated in his honor too, and both tragedy and comedy developed in Greece from the worship of Dionysus. The custom of sacrificing a goat on an altar in the marketplace was common as early as the seventh century B.C., and when theaters evolved the altar was retained. The great triad of fifth-century playwrights—Aeschylus, Sophocles, and Euripides—wrote plays for the Dionysiac and Lenaean festivals. These tragic poets are an important source of our knowledge of the Greek myths, which they used as metaphors or moral lessons to clarify some of the volatile issues of Athenian democracy. Euripides ascribed to the gods emotions and motives much like those of his own contemporaries, and he presented the cult of Dionysus as a religious choice—rich, frenzied, and irrational, as opposed to the serene and measured cult of Apollo. In *The Bacchants* Dionysus arrives in Thebes after planting his cult throughout Greece and Asia Minor. The chorus urges the Thebans to revel: to crown their heads with grapevines, drape themselves in fawnskins, and to riot, brandishing *thyrsi*—staffs made from the giant fennel plant capped with pine cones, grape or ivy leaves, or fruiting ivy stalks.

Dionysus and Maenads, after a black figure amphora from Vulci signed by the Amasis Painter, ca. 530 B.C. Paris, Bibliothèque Nationale.

Although Athens was greatly weakened politically and economically after the wars with Sparta, the fourth century B.C. was a time of unparalleled accomplishment in philosophy, art, and science. Theophrastus (c. 372–c. 287 B.C.), a pupil of both Plato and Aristotle, invented the character sketch, a prose form still in use today. In the dedicatory letter to his *Characters,* he marvels at the range of personality types to be found in a single nation. Three examples from *Characters* offer us not only Theophrastus on human nature in fourth-century Athens, but also reveal that the Greeks saw herbs as elements and metaphors of daily life:

> *Penuriousness* is an excessive economy of expenditure...this man is given to pressing for a debt and exacting usury upon usury; to setting small slices of meat before his fellow-citizens; to returning empty-handed from the market; and he will forbid his wife to lend a neighbor salt, or a lampwick, or aniseed, or marjoram, or barley groats, or incense, "for these little things come to so much in a year."

> *Superstitiousness*...would seem to be a sort of cowardice with respect to the divine (or spiritual) and your superstitious man is one who will not go out for the day till he has washed his hands and sprinkled himself at the Nine Springs, and put in his mouth a bit of bay leaf from a temple...

Parsimony is a neglect of honor when it involves expense...He will come home from the market carrying his own buyings of meat and pot–herbs in the folds of his gown.

Over the centuries the religious attitudes of Homer and Hesiod were challenged by new beliefs and cults and sometimes by the return of older practices. Although the Olympian gods gradually lost their mystery, their presence was felt through the centuries of decline in Greek power. Long after Greece became a part of the Roman empire, traditional Greek ideas and values persisted, reflected in the writings of men such as Plutarch, Epictetus, and Lucian.

The Greeks personified their gods in clear verbal and visual images, while the Romans expressed their relation to the gods in ritual acts. Grave, abstract powers of nature, the gods of the early Romans (sixth–fourth century B.C.) were not infused with the formal and poetic beauty of the Greek deities. There was no Olympus, no Hades, no genealogy of the gods, nor were there divine love affairs. A triumphal act performed with a laurel wreath by a man who represented the god Jupiter may best illustrate the Roman emphasis on ritual: during the festival of Jupiter, the god in his capacity as conqueror was represented by the Triumph (*triumphus,* from the Greek *thriambos,* a celebration in honor of Dionysus), who performed the ritual act by riding through the city in the insignia of the god—as Jupiter personified—in a procession to the Capitol, until the moment when he placed the laurel wreath of victory before the god's image.

Slowly the culture of Rome was altered by that of Greece, and by the first century B.C. the gods of Greece had in many ways merged with Roman deities. Amid the crises of the age of Caesar and Cicero, the brilliant Roman poet Catullus (84?–54 B.C.) compares a bride to the myrtle plant—a symbol of Venus, the Roman manifestation of Aphrodite—as he summons Hymen, the Greek god of marriage, to preside at a Roman wedding:

> Hymen, come, for Julia
> Weds with Manlius today,
>   And deigns to be a bride.
> Such a form as Venus wore
> In the contest famed of yore,
>   On Mount Ida's side;
> Like the myrtle or the bay,
> Florid, elegant, and gay,
>   With foliage fresh and new,
> Which the nymphs and forest maids
> Have fostered in sequestered shades,
>   With drops of holy dew.

Rejecting the concept of personal immortality and religious superstition, Lucretius (96?–55 B.C.) was the rare theorist among Roman thinkers. The first poet-scientist of nature, he constructed a bold, atomic explanation of the universe and of man's position within it. He followed the tradition of Greek philosophy before Socrates, one that began with Leucippus and Democritus and continued with Epicurus (341–270 B.C.), whose life, according to St. Jerome, was filled with "herbs, fruits, and abstinences."

The Pax Romana that accompanied the rule of Augustus inspired writers to celebrate and reaffirm the greatness of Rome. Virgil (Publius Virgilius Maro, 70–19 B.C.) completed his earliest poems, the *Eclogues,* in 37 B.C., ten years before Octavian received the title of Augustus. In the fourth eclogue Virgil speaks of "the newborn babe—who first shall end/That age of iron, bid a golden dawn/Upon the broad world..." and continues:

> On thee, child, everywhere shall earth, untilled,
> Show'r her first baby-offerings, vagrant stems
> Of ivy, foxglove, and gay briar, and bean;
> Unbid the goats shall come big-uddered home,
> Nor monstrous lions scare the herded kine.
> Thy cradle shall be full of pretty flowers:
> Die must the serpent, treacherous poison-plants
> Must die; and Syria's roses spring like weeds.

The pastoral manner begun by Virgil was adopted by another important Roman poet of the Augustan age, the tolerant, worldly Horace. He, like Virgil, was befriended by Maecenas, who gave the impoverished poet a small country estate in the Sabine district which allowed him to live the simple, agreeable life he preferred:

> Boy, I hate their empty shows;
>   Persian garlands I detest;
> Bring me not the late-blown rose
>   Lingering after all the rest.
>
>   * * * *
>
> Plainer myrtle pleases me
>   Thus outstretched beneath my vine—
> Myrtle more becoming thee
>   Waiting with thy master's wine.

Apollo and Daphne, after a Coptic textile, ca. sixth century A.D. Paris, Musée du Louvre.

Ovid (Publius Ovidius Naso, 43? B.C.–A.D. 17), the last great poet of the Augustan age, is a voluminous source for the classical myths. Ovid's myths are diverting stories, filled with secular wit and sentiment. In his masterpiece, the *Metamorphoses,* he tells the story of Apollo and Daphne, a myth that appears for the first time in antiquity. Apollo had long been in love with the mountain-nymph Daphne, and one day as she was hunting in the forest, he pursued her. The freedom-loving Daphne swiftly fled his advances, but he overtook her. Just as he touched her she cried out for help to her father, the river god Peneius, who transformed her into a laurel tree. To console himself, Apollo wove a wreath from the laurel leaves and so carried his love with him to share his future triumphs. The laurel remained his emblem, and the civilized pursuits of music, poetry, philosophy, and science were his provinces in classical times.

The forms of religious worship as well as the beliefs of the ancient Greeks and Romans were closely tied to the world of nature. Garlands of herbs sacred to the gods were offered on household and public altars, placed on the bodies and graves of the dead, and worn by the initiates at cult rituals. Although there was great diversity of belief over the fifteen hundred years from the time of Homer to the fall of Rome, many of the Greek myths and Roman rituals were designed to ensure abundance and well being. As a living form, the herb from earliest times was not only a real but a symbolic force both in religion and in healing.

I swear by Apollo...to reckon him who taught me this art equally dear to me as my parents...I will impart a knowledge of the art to my sons, and to those of my teachers ...I will give no deadly medicine to anyone if asked nor suggest such counsel...Into whatever houses I enter, I will go into them for the benefit of the sick, and will abstain from every voluntary act of mischief...Whatever...I see or hear, in the life of men... I will not divulge...

> Hippocrates (c. 460-370 B.C.), from the Hippocratic oath for new doctors

In considering the distinctive characters of plants and their nature generally, one must take into account their parts, their qualities, the ways in which their life originates, and the course it follows in each case.   Book I, I

Now since our study becomes more illuminating if we distinguish different kinds, it is well to follow this plan where it is possible. The first and foremost important classes, those which comprise all or nearly all plants, are tree, shrub, undershrub, herb.

> Theophrastus (c. 372-287 B.C.), *Enquiry into Plants,* Book I, III

Not even the woods and the wilder faces of Nature are without medicines, for there is no place where that holy Mother of all things did not distribute remedies for the healing of mankind, so that the very desert was made a drug store...

> Pliny (23-79), *Natural History,* Book XXIV, I

Obverse with a rose, silver tetradrachma from Rhodes, ca. 380/340 B.C.

MEDICINE, BOTANY, AND MAGIC

*C*lassical Greek medicine claimed as its divine precedents the healing gods Apollo and Asclepius, who was said to be Apollo's son by the mortal nymph Coronis. Apollo's sister Artemis slew Coronis for being unfaithful to her brother, but Apollo snatched the unborn Asclepius from the funeral pyre. He entrusted the child to the wise centaur Chiron who was celebrated for his knowledge of medicine and especially of herbs. After Asclepius had learned from Chiron the art of healing, Athena gave him supreme power, the Gorgon's blood, which he used several times to revive the dead. Jealous of such power, Zeus killed him with his thunderbolt, but through Apollo's intercession Asclepius was taken into the Olympian society of gods.

As a god Asclepius may derive from a pre-Greek divinity and so reflect herbal lore built up over many generations of folk healers. In the *Iliad,* Homer treats Asclepius as a mortal, a "blameless physician," whose sons Machaon and Podaleirus are also physicians in the Greek camp outside Troy. (At Troy Machaon himself suffers a shoulder wound, and Nestor, "the wisest of the Greeks," restores him with Pramnian wine and slices of onion and cheese.) To the physician in ancient Greece, Asclepius was both spiritual and physical ancestor, the source of the physician's art and profession which were handed down from father to son.

After the time of Homer, Asclepius became worshipped throughout the Greek world as the god of healing. In groves and medicinal springs sacred to him, cures were effected, and patients left votive tablets and offerings of thanks, detailing their complaints and cures. At his most famous temple in Epidaurus, a great festival to Asclepius with processions and combats was held every five years. According to Pliny the ancients knew several varieties of a medicinal plant called *panaces* (a cure for all diseases) said to have been discovered by Asclepius and his teacher Chiron. The first was *panaces asclepion,* for which Asclepius named his daughter Panacea. The discovery of *panaces chironium* and *panaces centaurion* was attributed to Chiron.

Medicine mingled with magic both early and late in ancient Greece. Both relied greatly on herbs. In classical Greece, however, many Greek doctors, such as Hippocrates of Cos (c. 460–370 B.C.), replaced magical cures with direct observation, dietary control, and nursing care. The useful practices that resulted led to a true science of medicine with a vital development until late antiquity.

Hippocrates, the most famous of Greek physicians, is considered the father of modern medicine, although little is actually known of him. He abandoned the old beliefs in supernatural cures to develop a system based on scientific method that included a careful examination of each patient's history and symptoms before diagnosis and treatment. Most of Hippocrates' *materia medica* came from the plant world, and he left a list of several hundred herbal simples (herbs used singly as cures). Some of the herbs he prescribed are still in general use today, such as coriander, garlic, mint, sage, rosemary, and thyme. The noxious animal compounds used before and after his time were omitted entirely. In *The Science of Medicine*—a defense of medical practices of the time—the true physician is considered one who uses not only drugs and purges as therapeutic measures but also other regimens such as diet.

> There is nothing done by good doctors which is useless, nor is there anything useless in the science of medicine. The majority of plants and preparations contain substances of a remedial or pharmaceutical nature and no one who is cured without the service of a doctor can ascribe his cure to chance.

Included in the *Regimen in Acute Diseases* is a prescription for a purge that was universal in ancient Greece: either black hellebore or purple spurge, adding to the black hellebore parsnip, seseli, cumin, anise, or some other fragrant herb, and to the purple spurge the juice of *silphium* (see page 30). The *Regimen* also refers to a group of therapeutic drinks made from barley, herbs, raisins or the second pressing of grapes, wheat, thistle or myrtle, and pomegranates. Wines or mixtures of wine, herbs, and water, and abstention from either or both, are spelled out in careful detail for specific illnesses.

Another renowned Greek physician, Diocles of Carystos (375?–300? B.C.), was the first known author of a Greek herbal. A contemporary of Aristotle, whom he may have influenced, Diocles produced a work on medical botany no longer extant, consisting of descriptions of plants employed at the time and their habitats, followed by a list of medicinal uses.

The first systematic analysis of the plant world was made by Theophrastus (c. 372–c. 287 B.C.), successor to Aristotle and co-founder of the Lyceum. His constant question in the *Enquiry into Plants* is, "How does this plant differ from others?" Born in Lesbos, he came to be the favorite pupil of Aristotle. When Aristotle died, he left his books and his garden on the Lyceum grounds to Theophrastus, who made many of his botanical observations there. Not only did Theophrastus classify all plants as trees, shrubs, undershrubs, or herbs, but he noted their geography and environment, their propagation and growth characteristics, as well as their medicinal properties.

Theophrastus defines an herb as a plant that comes up from the root with its leaves and has no main stem; its seeds are carried on the stems. He is constantly wary of being too rigid in his definitions; some pot-herbs, he observes, even come to have a tree-like shape; and he suggests that in some cases we should classify simply by size, or comparative hardiness, or length of life. He then details the sowing times of different herbs, and the germination periods of their seeds: dill and mustard (5 days), long onion (10–12), leeks (19–20), savory and marjoram (more than 30), celery (40–50), and coriander germinates with difficulty. Again, Theophrastus sees variables—differences in the seeds themselves, the ground, atmosphere, season, or weather. One generalization he allows: that all herbs love water and manure.

Herbs as medicines are the subject of Book IX of Theophrastus' *Enquiry*, and in it he outlines the kinds and parts of plants used, the methods of collecting their juices, and their effects on humans and animals. He also gives examples of some scientific and superstitious herbal practices. The advice of druggists and herb-diggers to curse and abuse cumin when planting the seeds to ensure an abundant crop, for example, he finds irrelevant. On the other hand, he endorses those customs he finds valid: gather the fruit of the wild rose standing into the wind to avoid harm to the eyes, or eat garlic with undiluted wine when digging hellebore to prevent heaviness in the head.

Toward the end of the third century B.C. in republican Rome, Cato the Elder (234–149), a statesman and author renowned for his devotion to old Roman ideals, wrote *On Agriculture (De agri cultura)*, a practical treatise on farming and country life. Based on first-hand experience, it is written in the severely simple style of a farmer's notebook. It gives directions on selecting and caring for land, cattle, and slaves; building a house, stalls, and pens; choosing an overseer and equipment; planting grain, vineyards, olive trees, and vegetables; making wine and olive oil; and using herbs. Among the instructions for a farm near a town is the recommendation that a garden be planted with all types of vegetables, as well as flowers for making garlands—Megarian bulbs, conjugulan myrtle, white and black myrtle, Delphian, Cyprian, and wild laurel. Cato's many wine recipes include a wine for ordinary drinking made with aromatic herbs and another wine for curing indigestion and colic made with black and white myrtle. A preventive for illness in oxen, that was to be prepared and administered by someone only while standing and after fasting, calls for 3 grains of salt; 3 leaves each of laurel, leek, and rue; 3 spikes each of leek and garlic; 3 grains of incense; 3 Sabine herb plants; 3 stalks of bryony; 3 white beans; 3 live coals; and 3 pints of wine. This prescription seems to be a very Roman blend of magic, superstition, and medicine.

Another Roman author, Marcus Terentius Varro (116–27 B.C.), wrote on almost every known subject. Only one work of the estimated 620 volumes written by Varro remains intact, his *On Agriculture (De re rustica)*, begun in his eightieth year and dedicated to his wife who had just bought a farm. Between the setting of the Pleiades and the winter solstice Varro advises "the planting of lilies and crocus," and "a rose which has already formed a root is cut from the root up into twigs a palm-breadth long and planted." He also refers to a plant nursery *(seminarium)* on the farm, remarking that "wild lemon thyme *(serpyllum)* gets its name from the fact that it creeps, and it should be transplanted from the nursery between the beginning of the west wind to the rising of Arcturus." Varro writes at length on beekeeping, an important Roman industry, as honey was used universally not only as a food and a preservative but as a component of many medicines. An apiary needs an agreeable spot near food and water, and if there is no natural food, "sow crops most attractive to the bees: rose, wild thyme, balm, poppy, bean, lentil, pea, clover, rush, alfalfa, and snail-clover [for sick bees], but thyme is best-suited to honey-making."

Virgil too gives instructions on the best location for beehives in the last section of the *Georgics*. They should be in a sheltered spot, near running springs and a slender brook, shaded by palm trees or wild olives; and the farmer should make piers from heavy rocks and boughs as resting places for the bees; and he should: "Plant laurels all around, and fragrant thyme; set out a crop of pungent savory, and violet beds to drink the trickling spring."

It was a first-century Roman, however, who wrote most voluminously on the history, botany, and uses of plants and herbs. Pliny the Elder (Gaius Plinius Secundus, A.D. 23–79), left an encyclopedia of the Roman world, in thirty-seven books, which treats some 33,000 subjects. Seven of the thirty-seven volumes of his *Natural History,* or *History of the World (Naturalis historia)* are devoted to medical botany. Born in Como and trained as a lawyer and orator, Pliny served in the army in Germany and went to Spain in charge of revenue under Vespasian. He was serving as prefect of the fleet at Misenum under Titus in A.D. 79 when he saw a cloud that "looked like an umbrella pine" over Vesuvius. Pliny sailed off immediately to investigate the eruption and later died at the scene, asphyxiated by the sulphurous fumes from the volcano.

Although Pliny gave many, many pages to superstitious and apocryphal tales, he is among those educated first-century Romans who rejected popular religion and mythology. An indefatigably active observer of his surroundings, Pliny saw divinity and nature as inseparable. In other ways he was a latter-day Cato, praising natural practices and hard work—the old Roman ideals. He was extremely critical of the fads and excesses of Roman physicians and chefs, and he resoundingly damned the practice of magic. It was extraordinary to him that medicine and magic could have flourished together in Greece, that Democritus could have advocated magic at the same time Hippocrates advocated medicine; and, he added, a tremendous debt was owed the Romans for eradicating magic in Italy. Yet, magic appears not to have vanished, for in the book on trees he reports that the emperor Tiberius would wear a laurel wreath whenever it thundered to avoid being struck by lightning.

While references to herbs occur in twenty-seven of Pliny's thirty-seven books, discussions of garden or medicinal herbs are concentrated in books nineteen through twenty-seven. Book XIX begins with an elaborate exposition on the wonderful audacities man has perpetrated with agriculture such as conquering the world with a tiny flaxseed: from the flax came linen for weaving and from the linen, sails for ships made of wood from the forests, ships that crossed the seas to subdue other peoples. Pliny then moves to the cultivation of kitchen gardens, a subject he views with both affection and respect. Not only do garden plants offer healthful food for the price of cultivation, but also remedies for diseases at little or no cost. The pursuit of gardening itself, he observes, was thought to promote longevity.

In his discussion of the medicinal values of wine, Pliny comments on one of the most innovative and appreciated physicians of ancient times, Asclepiades of Prusa, who practiced in Rome during the first century B.C. His medical doctrine was based on a theory of atoms, in contrast to the theories of Hippocrates and later of Galen. Influenced by Epicurean philosophy, Asclepiades explained health as the free movement of bodily corpuscles, and disease as their inhibited movement. Diet rather than drugs was his therapy, and the job of the physician was to cure safely, speedily, and pleasantly *(tuto, celeriter, iucunde)*. Pliny refers to a book by Asclepiades on the use of wine which led him to be nicknamed "the wine-giver," although his commentators later wrote an endless number of books on the medicinal uses of wine. Asclepiades asserted, Pliny continues, that the usefulness of wine is hardly exceeded by the power of the gods.

Despite the strong tendency to rely on foreign novelties and to ignore native plants, the Romans attributed an astonishing number of remedies to vegetables, including the herb-vegetables onion and garlic. Herbs used for flavoring also had medicinal values: eighty-four remedies were given to rue, sixty-six to the mints, sixty-one to anise, and forty-four to mustard. Garlic, for example, was thought to be of positive benefit against changes of water and locale. It kept serpents at bay and, some claimed, all other animals, too. It was a cure for bites—including those from shrew-mice and dogs—when drunk, eaten, or applied as ointment. Mashed and drunk with vinegar it was used as a gargle for quinsy, mixed with salt and oil it relieved sprains and ruptures, and when pounded with fresh coriander and taken in wine it was believed to act as an aphrodisiac. Although Pliny stated his preference for native herbal simples, he nevertheless listed thousands of the disdained foreign prescriptions: plant mixtures, animal remedies, cures of professional physicians. Despite his abhorrence of the more blatant forms of superstition and magic, Pliny seems to have accepted the milder forms from his own heritage of popular medicine in Italy.

If Pliny's encyclopedia lacked practicality as a medical textbook, the field observations of Pedanius Dioscorides (first century A.D.)—a contemporary unknown to Pliny, from Anazarba, Greece—became a reference manual used by physicians for the next fifteen hundred years. It was the medieval physician's duty to "fear God and know his Dioscorides," and the modern science of pharmacology stems from his attempts to systematize medical knowledge. As a surgeon in the Roman army, Dioscorides made his observations in the field; and at the suggestion of a fellow-physician later compiled his *De materia medica* (c. A.D. 65), a five-part treatise containing remedies from about 500 plants. He also recommended about seventy animal remedies, among them two made with vipers' flesh—long celebrated as a poison antidote. This snake meat pickled in oil, wine, salt, and dill was recommended for sharpening eyesight and for nerves. A remedial delicacy of viper roasted with salt, honey, figs, and spikenard had a long popularity and later was made into a soup still favored in Europe.

Dioscorides cataloguing the mandrake in his herbal, from an early sixth century A.D. manuscript. Vienna, Nationalbibliothek.

The oldest known version of Dioscorides' *materia medica* is included in a manuscript illustrated by a Byzantine artist about A.D. 512 for presentation to Juliana Anicia, daughter of Anicius Olybrius, a former emperor of the West *(Codex Vindobonensis Med.* Gr. I, Vienna). Some of the illustrations seem to be based on those of Crateuas, a pharmacologist at the court of Mithridates (111–64 B.C.), who wrote two works now lost. One was a comprehensive scientific study on medicines, the other a more popular book of colored illustrations of plants, annotated with their medical uses. Because Crateuas' pictures were thought so lifelike, he is considered the father of botanical illustration.

A century after Dioscorides, another physician-writer left no area of medicine untouched in his more than 200 volumes on anatomy, physiology, pharmacology, and therapeutics. Claudius Galenus (c. A.D. 130–200), or Galen, was born in Pergamon and educated there and in Smyrna, Corinth, and Alexandria. Returning to Pergamon in 158, he became physician to a gladiatorial school to gain surgical knowledge. From about the year 162 he worked chiefly in Rome where he established a large medical practice, lectured on anatomy, and carried out experiments that included animal dissection. In Rome he was court physician to Marcus Aurelius and later private physician to Commodus. While his work in anatomy and physiology was especially important and his authority in these areas almost unchallenged until the sixteenth century, the term *galenic* refers particularly to his principles and practices regarding the use of plant preparations as distinguished from chemical ones. A galenical is a vegetable remedy or an herbal simple.

Paralleling the tremendous development of a science and profession of medicine during antiquity was the tradition of folk medical lore. Often professional and popular medicine were used together. If the origins of both medicine and magic remain obscure to us, we can assume that perhaps primitive man first treated himself—with the plant and animal material around him—until the "medicine man" appeared to superimpose incantations and taboos. Only later did the classical Greeks combine systematic observation with non-mystical causal theory to bring about scientific medicine. None of these approaches excluded the others in the ancient world. Many people ignored or disdained physicians and scientific medicine, preferring the faith cures of popular healers or those remedies that could be self-administered. With the decline of the Roman empire the sciences were eclipsed, the medical profession almost vanished, and herbal medicine was tenuously kept alive by Christian monks who preserved the manuscripts of Dioscorides, Pliny, and Galen.

Outside the courtyard, near the entrance, is a great garden of four acres with a fence bordering it on each side. Here tall, thriving trees are planted—pears, pomegranates, apples with glistening fruit, sweet figs, rich olives. The fruit of these trees never fails in any season of the year, for here the west wind is always breathing—generating some fruits and ripening others. Pear upon pear matures to fullness, apple on apple, grape-cluster upon grape-cluster, fig on fig. There too the king has his fruitful vineyard planted; behind is a warm and level spot, dried by the sun, where some grapes are being gathered and others trodden; in front there are unripe grapes that have scarcely shed their blossoms, and others already faintly darkening. There, too, bordering the last row of vines, are trim plots of all kinds of herbs that stay green throughout the year. There are also two springs of water, and one of these is channelled out over the entire garden; the other, facing it, flows under the entrance of the courtyard to issue in front of the lofty palace; and from it the townspeople draw their water.

The Odyssey VII, The Garden of Alcinous

Around the entrance a deep wood rose up in summer growth—alder and poplar and fragrant cypress. Birds with long wings roosted there, owls and falcons, long-tongued cormorants—beachcombers and water followers. Trailing over the smooth-walled cave was a thriving vine with purple flowers; and here four springs arose near each other, and then channelled their crystal waters through grassy meadows thick with violet and wild parsley. Even a god, if he came there, might gaze in wonder at the sight and feel a sense of delight, as Hermes did...

The Odyssey V, The Garden of Calypso

Crocus plants on a terracotta conical rhyton found at Akrotiri on Thera, ca. 1600-1500 B.C. Athens, National Museum.

HOUSE AND GARDEN

Greek and Roman houses and gardens reflected the religious values of their owners. Both houses and gardens had altars to favorite or family gods, and the gardens also provided herbs for the medicine chest and kitchen as well as herbs and flowers for the interior altars or images. The idea of gardens grew from early religion and legend.

Two early types of Greek gardens are known. Pierre Grimal in *Les Jardins Romains* distinguishes the formal sacred gardens surrounding Greek sanctuaries and the freer, more natural, sacred groves associated with some of the Olympian gods. Both may have originated in the pre-Greek vegetation cults of the Aegean world. These two garden types, as well as a third kind—the bountiful palace garden of Alcinous visited by Odysseus—inspired garden design throughout the Mediterranean world until the end of the Roman empire. Alcinous' garden was a symbol of perpetual abundance, an ideal picture of rustic simplicity and fertility worthy of the heroic age. The image was kept alive by the Alexandrian pastoral poets and later in Rome by Virgil and Horace. But the sacred groves of the gods had an even stronger effect on the subsequent development of historic gardens. The attraction of these groves was in their natural beauty rather than in their fruitfulness, in their foliage, flowers, and grottoes only slightly enhanced by artifice and symmetry.

There is little evidence for domestic gardens in archaic and classical Greek towns and cities. The urban houses of ordinary Greek citizens usually had small interior courts, particularly in Athens where residential areas were severely compacted, streets very narrow, and water in short supply. These courtyards were not planted but were of beaten earth or paved with cobblestones, cement, or mosaics—more open-air rooms than garden spots. Gardens that produced specialty foods and herbs, however, existed just outside the city walls. Potted plants are known, but mostly in connection with festivals like the Adonia, where women mourned the death of Adonis, Aphrodite's lover, by setting out pots planted with quick-growing seeds such as fennel and grasses, the generation of which symbolized rebirth, spring after winter.

By the fifth century B.C. the royal gardens of Persia, especially the *paradeisos* of Cyrus at Sardis, were imitated by some wealthy Greeks. The fashion took hold in Hellenistic times, and the imitation of Oriental gardens persisted throughout antiquity. Grimal suggests, however, that it was the more natural "sacred grove" tradition that led to the development of parks in Greece. The Academy in Athens was the most famous of these parks, an open-air gymnasium of the archaic period dedicated to military maneuvers as well as to other physical and mental exercise. Its name derived from Academus, an obscure hero whose worship was associated with that of Prometheus and Hephaestus.

Maenads before an image of Dionysus, from a stamnos by the Dinos Painter, ca. 420 B.C. Naples, Museo Nazionale.

Plutarch writes that during the time of Pericles, Cimon planted the Agora with plane trees and changed "the Academy from a waterless and arid spot into a well-watered grove, which he provided with clear running tracks and shady walks"—plantings no longer related to ritual but intended now for enjoyment. Plato established his school on a property adjacent to the shrine, and the school adopted the name of the park itself; there teacher and students strolled in the shade of the trees. A generation later Aristotle founded his own school in the Lyceum, another park-like gymnasium in the eastern suburbs of Athens; and later Epicurus began to teach in his urban garden. At the end of the first century B.C. these philosophic parks still existed in Athens, models to be imitated by the Romans. Among all the gardens of Greece and the Orient they were especially admired because of their link with the Greek past.

The Romans had a deep and enduring affection for gardens, which were an intimate part of their spiritual and physical lives. In Roman law the family house, orchard, and kitchen garden were thought of as an inseparable unit of inherited property. A number of ancient divinities were worshipped as guardians of the garden: Varro advises invocation of the twelve councillor gods, but not "those urban gods whose images stand around the forum bedecked with gold, six male and a like number of females, but those twelve gods who are special patrons of the husbandmen." He then invokes Jupiter and Tellus, "the Father" and "Mother Earth," who through sky and earth embrace all the fruits of agriculture, Sol and Luna whose courses are watched in all matters of planting and harvesting, Ceres and Liber by whose favor food and drink come to the farm, Robigus and Flora who keep harmful rust from the grain and trees, Minerva and Venus who protect the oliveyard and garden, and finally Lympha and Bonus Eventus who keep the ground moist and fertile. The Greek personification of fertility, Priapus, became in Rome the protector of the garden, his statue serving both as scarecrow and guardian.

Growth of the Roman population caused a decline of the small produce garden and brought about its replacement by scientific market-gardening. Huge quantities of vegetables had to be produced for the metropolitan area, and in the adjacent rural regions whole fields became gardens. In the first century B.C. Varro observed that all of Italy looked like a garden.

In her comprehensive work *The Gardens of Pompeii,* Dr. Wilhelmina Jashemski clearly establishes the importance of gardens in the daily lives of the Romans. She found that within the irregular oval of Pompeii's walls gardens appear in the most unexpected places and that over one-third of the excavated city is open space. About half this open space was used for streets and forums, and the other for cultivation—9.7% for large food-producing areas, 5.4% for house gardens, and 2.6% for gardens of public or business buildings.

In the House of the Surgeon of the late fourth or early third century B.C. in Pompeii, a modest garden occupied an area at the rear within the perimeter walls of the building. By the second century B.C., houses of wealthy Samnites had become larger, higher, and more luxurious, in accord with the Hellenistic peristyle architecture of the time. The Greek peristyle—or colonnaded open space—functions much like the Roman atrium, as an open court leading to surrounding rooms. When the Italians added the peristyle to the atrium plan of their houses, the Hellenistic peristyle courtyard became a garden. Yet, to date, there is no evidence of a planted peristyle in ancient Greek houses. To one side of the peristyle in the House of the Silver Wedding in Pompeii was another garden, large and secluded, for family meals in summer. Many small channels in the garden carried water that spilled over the fountain to the plants, and the shape of the planting beds indicates that this was a vegetable and herb garden in which flowers and fruit trees also grew. A humbler house in southeast Pompeii had a garden with grape vines, four large trees, and a number of smaller orchard trees. The widely spaced trees and the discovery of carbonized fava beans in this garden suggest that vegetables and herbs would have been grown among the trees.

In the *Natural History,* Pliny describes the layout of a typical Roman kitchen garden that, as Dr. Jashemski observes, clearly coincides with another Pompeiian garden. After giving directions for preparing the soil, Pliny recommends marking out the land in plots bordered by sloping, rounded banks and surrounded by furrowed paths for the gardener's access, as well as a channel for irrigation. One of the most important Pompeiian houses of the Samnite period is the House of Pansa, which occupied an entire city block. The house had a large atrium, a splendid peristyle garden, and behind it a colonnade that

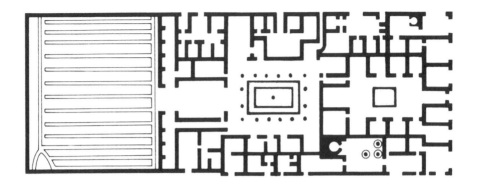

Plan of the House of Pansa, Pompeii, ca. second Century B.C.

looked onto a garden one-third the area of the total building plot, or *insula.* A plan was drawn by the French scholar Mazois at the time of the excavation, when the planting arrangement of the garden was perfectly preserved. His layout of the garden not only is the same one Pliny recommended, but it is the same plan used today for produce gardens in the environs of Pompeii.

Among the garden trees and plants that occur in Greek and Roman literature as well as in ancient wall painting and sculptural decoration are the acanthus, ivy, laurel, myrtle, olive, rose, and lily. While only the descendants of the plants of that era survive, specialists in the past few decades have gained much new information on the ancient plants themselves from their study of carbonized plant remains, as well as from ancient root cavities and soil from excavations. A 1974 find at Torre Annunziata in Campania has been published by Dr. Jashemski. Several cubic meters of carbonized plant material were discovered in a room off the peristyle of the villa of L. Crassus Tertius. Of the 111 taxonomic entities identified thus far from this material, sixty-seven species, thirty-seven genera, and one family have been added to the list of 408 plants that were probably known and used in the first century A.D. This is the first such find of actual vegetation on the land of a villa, although the agricultural importance of villa gardens has been clear from both literary and archaeological evidence.

Except in ancient Sparta, agriculture was considered a dignified occupation for a Greek freedman from Homeric times until at least the second century B.C. While Thessaly was largely tilled by serfs, Attica was made up of small estates, and their yield, or its monetary equivalent, determined the social status of the owner. During the fifth and fourth centuries agriculture became progressively more scientific with the adoption of such advanced practices as crop rotation. The vine, fig, and olive were particularly suited to the stony Greek countryside, and near Athens herbs and vegetables were cultivated in quantity.

In the ancient Mediterranean world the pleasures of eating varied from rural subsistence to urban gourmandizing. Both in Greece and in Rome, every century heard warnings on dietary excesses from physicians, philosophers, statesmen, and poets. Until the middle of the fifth century B.C., all Greeks ate much the same simple foods. We know from literary sources beginning with Homer that the Greeks cultivated herbs. Among those they used for seasoning were anise, basil, coriander, cumin, dill, fennel, savory, and saffron. As Athens reached its height in the late fifth century, the diets of rich and poor diverged. No Greek cookbooks have survived, but we know a few authors' names, titles, and fragments. Glocis of Locris wrote on cooking as an art, Aegis of Rhodes specialized in roast fish, Nereus of Chios prepared conger eel worthy of the gods, and Aristion planned gourmet picnics. The first of the writers on food was Archestratus, who lived in the fourth century B.C. and travelled extensively to test and to share the delights of his gastronomic adventures. Archestratus is quoted often in a collection of excerpts and anecdotes called the *Deipnosophistai* (Sophists at Dinner, or, Connoisseurs in Dining) by Athenaeus of Naucratis who wrote in the third century A.D. Archestratus talks of a banquet in Book III:

> And always at the banquet crown your head
> With flowing wreaths of varied scent and hue,
> Culling the treasures of the happy earth;
> and steep your hair in rich and pungent odors,
> And all day long pour holy frankincense
> and Myrrh, the fragrant fruit of Syria,
> on the slow slumb'ring ashes of the fire:
> Then when you drink let the slaves these luxuries bring—
> Tripe, and the boiled paunch of well-fed swine,
> Well soak'd in cummin juice and vinegar,
> And sharp, strong smelling asafoetida;
> Taste, too, the tender well-roast birds, and game,
> Whate'er may be in season.
> All other foods are only signs
> Of wretched poverty: the green boiled vetch,
> And beans and apples, and dried drums of figs.
> But praise the cheesecakes which from Athens come;
> And if there are none, still of any country
> Cheesecakes are to be eaten; also ask
> For Attic honey, the feast's crowning dish—
> For that it is which makes a banquet noble.

Archestratus is a Greek, however, and he prefers a more natural fare, noting elsewhere that bonita is excellent prepared in many different ways, but it is best when wrapped in a fig leaf and baked under the ashes, without cheese or any other seasoning. Antiphanes (408–334 B.C.), an outstanding playwright and a contemporary of Archestratus, comments on a sparser Greek diet of the fourth century:

Our supper is but maize well fenced round
With chaff, so as not to o'erstep the bounds
Of well-devised economy. An onion,
A few side dishes, and a sow-thistle,
A mushroom, or what wild and tasteless roots
The place offers us in our poverty.
Such is our life, not much exposed to fevers;
For no one when there's meat, will eat of Thyme,
Not even the pupils of Pythagoras.

Even the garden pest left his poetic mark in a fragment by the Athenian comic poet Strattis (active late fourth-century B.C.):

The leek-destroying grubs, which go
Throughout the leafy gardens
On fifty feet, and leave their trace,
Gnawing all herbs and vegetables;
Leading the dances of the long-tailed satyrs
Amid the petals of the verdant herbs
And of the juicy lettuces
And of the fragrant parsley.

Roman food was essentially an elaboration of Greek food. Under Greek influence the Romans began to eat bread more than the old-fashioned pastes and porridges. For the wealthy Romans spices and seasonings became a requirement of fine cooking. The Roman poor, however, ate *puls* (a porridge of millet or barley), grain paste, or coarse bread, and with it probably olives and cheese. Beets, beans, sorrel, and cabbage commonly augmented this basic diet. The middle class Roman in the first century A.D. could add to this fish, eggs, some meat, fruits, and wine.

Imperial Roman extravagance may have been at its most absurd in the cuisine and eating habits of the ostentatious rich. Certainly it was a cuisine of considerable sophistication, although many of the recipes that come down to us lack precise proportions and thus are difficult to evaluate. We do know that the number and kinds of ingredients available to wealthy Romans were staggering, and that there was a constant search for new culinary sensations. Foods and condiments from foreign lands were especially appealing: oysters from Britain, pickles from Spain, preserved fruits from Syria or Asia, spices from India and Arabia. Even wines were imported, despite the excellent ones produced at home. Virgil started to enumerate the wines he knew, in his *Georgics* (II), but abandoned the attempt. Pliny in the next century enumerated about a hundred local and foreign varieties and then concluded that they were numberless. Many rich Romans preferred their food to look and taste like what it was not: one famous recipe invented in an inland city used a ground walnut paste to counterfeit a herring. To transform the flavors of foods, a formidable number of herbs and spices was used, often in potent combinations. In addition to the spices imported from the Orient, the Romans made daily use of herbs from local gardens, especially basil, dill, lovage, mint, oregano, parsley, rue, savory, and thyme. Anise, bay, fennel, poppy, and sesame seeds were standard flavorings for breads and cakes.

There were liquid seasonings as well, and the most common were *garum* and *liquamen*. Originally distinct sauces, they became virtually synonymous by the late Roman empire. *Garum* was a sauce made of salted, fermented fish to which herbs and other ingredients such as wine and spices might be added during fermentation. Although *garum* could be mixed with many other ingredients, four types were used extensively. The four basic mixtures were made with water *(hydrogarum)*, oil *(oleogarum)*, vinegar *(oxygarum)*, and wine *(oenogarum)*. *Garum* was known as early as the fifth century B.C. in Greece, but it came into use in Italy much later. Once it arrived there, it became a universal ingredient, used in every sauce for fish, meat, fowl, and vegetables. It was, for example, combined with pepper, pine nuts, and asafoetida to season the stuffing for baked dormouse *(Glis glis)*, a Roman delicacy so valued that the Romans designed a special environment, a *gliraria,* to ensure a ready supply of dormice fattened on chestnuts, acorns, and walnuts.

It was only a short step from the ingenuity of such a creation to the banquets described by Roman emperors, gastronomes, and writers. Gluttony and exhibitionism sometimes went hand-in-hand, and the sumptuary laws instituted during the republic were repeatedly revised to curb excesses. Limitations were placed on the number of animals that could be slaughtered for festivals, games, and weddings, as well as on how much silverware could be used. Some laws permitted the consumption of only native wines, rather than imported vintages. During the dictatorship of Sulla, for example, three hundred sesterces could be spent lawfully on dinners for festal occasions, but no more than thirty on any others. An Aemilian law of 78 B.C. restricted the kind and quality of food that could be served. In the time of Augustus, the Julian law set still tougher limits: a thousand sesterces could be spent for weddings, three hundred for holidays, and two hundred for working days. Yet, although they were often revised, these laws were constantly violated and their enforcers frequently invited to join the party.

Cicero (106–43 B.C.) points out in a letter the grave error of exempting vegetables from sumptuary control. At a banquet he attended the cooks had prepared such delicious gourmet dishes of "mushrooms, root vegetables, and all kinds of herbs" that Cicero was indisposed for more than ten days after. "So I, who have no difficulty in abstaining from oysters and lampreys, was caught out by beets and mallow."

Only one cookbook survives from ancient Greece and Rome, a late fourth- or early fifth-century compilation called the *De re coquinaria.* It is associated with Marcus Gavius Apicius, a rich gastronome of the time of Augustus and Tiberius. Whether he was a glutton or a gourmet is still disputed. Many of Apicius' recipes were famous and many others were named after him, according to Athenaeus, including several cheesecakes.

The Apician recipes themselves are tantalizing to the modern palate. Some of them are impractical, or even undecipherable, but others are quite adaptable to present cooking methods. The compilation begins with instructions to the Careful Experienced Cook on preserving foods and herbs, a subject of real concern before refrigeration. It continues with sections on The Gardener, Legumes, Poultry, Quadrupeds, and Seafood. Fish Sauces and Fancy Dishes also receive special treatment.

Herbs are used throughout Apicius—from the first recipe for spiced wine to the last recipe for eel sauce. Herbs are integrated in all foods, even in a raisin nut custard. They are used as salad greens and vegetables with dressings of their own and as whisks to flavor sauces. Bay, coriander, cumin, dill, leek, lovage, mint, myrtle berries, onions, oregano, parsley, rue, thyme, and many others appear again and again along with pepper, *garum,* and *silphium. Silphium* was an expensive, highly prized herb from Cyrene that disappeared due to overharvesting about the time of Nero when the costly Persian asafoetida was substituted for it.

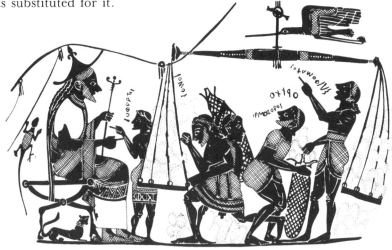

Weighing and storing of food for shipment, from a Laconian cup by the Arkesilas Painter, ca. 565-560 B.C. Paris, Bibliothèque Nationale.

An Apician recipe could be as simple as liberally peppering radishes or as complicated as *Pisa farsilis* (freely translated, Peas Supreme) which calls for several dozen ingredients, an herbal white sauce, and a silver platter (see page 63). Seneca and Martial tell the story of Apicius' end. Having spent much of his fortune on gourmandizing, Apicius still had one-sixth of it left. Fearing a simpler life, he is said to have poisoned himself at a banquet designed for the occasion. Martial's epigram *To Apicius* reads:

> You had spent sixty thousand on gorging your fill,
> And there only remained a poor ten thousand still.
> That to you was starvation; so into your cup
> You poured deadly poison and drank the lot up.
> You were always a gourmet, of that I am sure;
> But by death you were proven the complete epicure.

One of the most celebrated Roman banquets was Trimalchio's dinner in the *Satyricon* by Petronius, and its author also committed suicide in style. Petronius (d. 66) was an indolent and luxury-loving gentleman, so discerning of refinement that he was made *Arbiter elegantiae* at the court of Nero. There he directed the emperor's entertainment until he was sabotaged by a jealous rival. In the best prose style of the time, interspersed with verse, the *Satyricon* is a triumph of realism that satirizes the vulgar display of the *nouveaux riches* of the early empire. Trimalchio is a freedman of new wealth and his dinner an outlandish parody of magnificence—its inventions correspond perfectly to his own pompous view of luxury. After elaborate *trompe l'oeil* appetizers, a one-hundred-year-old wine was served as a slave displayed a moveable silver skeleton to the guests—wine and skeleton were double symbols of ostentatious wealth and mortality. The dinner continues apace:

> Around a circular tray were the twelve signs of the Zodiac and upon each sign the chef had placed the most appropriate food. Chick peas on the sign of Aries, on Taurus a piece of beef, lamb kidneys and testicles on Gemini, a crown of flowers on Cancer, on Leo an African fig, virgin sow belly on Virgo, on Libra a scale with a tart in one pan and a cheese cake in the other, on Scorpio a crawfish, on Capricorn a lobster, on Aquarius a goose, and two mullets on Pisces. In the center was a honeycomb atop a clump of turf still green with grass. A long-haired black slave handed out bread from a silver chafing dish as he shrilled a song from the musical farce *Asafoetida*. Seeing our reluctance to deal with this bizarre fare, Trimalchio kept urging: "Eat up, gentlemen, this is only the sauce."
>
> Chapter xxxv

BASIL

τὸ βασιλικόν

(basilikón)

Ocimum

*B*asil has been a controversial herb from ancient times. Both the origin of its name and its reason for being have been constantly disputed. The Greek *basilikón*, means "kingly," while the Latin *ocimum* may derive from the Greek ἡ ὄσφρησις ("the sense of being able to enjoy the fragrance"), because of the plant's pungent aroma. In ancient Greece it was thought that basil represented hate and misfortune. The Greeks called it the "devil plant," but they also considered it a powerful love charm. A sign of mourning in ancient Greece and a sign of love in ancient Rome, today in Crete basil signifies "love washed with tears," and in some parts of Italy it remains a lover's emblem.

Sweet basil (*Ocimum basilicum*) was a staple of the ancient Greek kitchen garden and many Greeks believed that it would not grow unless it was cursed and reviled when planted. Aristotle's colleague Theophrastus disagreed, having observed the habits of herbs scientifically. Each of the kitchen herbs he studied flowered all at once, except basil, which produces a succession of flowers starting at the lower part of the plant. He also observed that basil produces more seeds than do other herbs. Pliny in the first century reported the belief still accepted by many Romans that the more basil was abused, the more abundantly it grew, and that the best time for sowing was at the Feast of Pales on April 21. At the rising of the Dog Star, he added, basil turns pale.

The medicinal values of basil were also disputed in antiquity. According to Pliny, the Greek botanist-physician Chrysippus condemned it, claiming that it injured stomach, liver, and eyes, and that it even caused madness, which explained why goats would not touch it. Other authorities added that pounded basil placed under a stone would breed a scorpion. Dioscorides and Pliny rescued basil. Dioscorides recommends it for intestinal worms, mad dog and viper bites, dandruff, and toothache; he also includes instructions for making an ointment of basil leaves pounded in oil. Pliny refutes the more exaggerated negatives and catalogues the herb's benefits: mixed with wine and a little vinegar, basil cures the sting of land and sea scorpions; mixed with vinegar and inhaled it is good for fainting; as a linament with rose oil and vinegar it relieves fatigue, inflammation, and headache; when mixed with goose grease it is especially good for babies' ears; it is also an aphrodisiac.

Apicius, a rich gastronome of Pliny's time, is associated with the only known cookbook from ancient Greece or Rome (see page 30). In it is a recipe for fresh or dried peas (*De pisis*) seasoned with herbs and wine:

> Cook peas and skim the broth. Add leeks, coriander, and cumin. Pound pepper, lovage, caraway, dill, and fresh basil, and moisten with *liquamen*. Blend the herbs

Ocimum basilicum Linnaeus. *Labiatae.*

with additional *liquamen* and wine. Add to peas and taste, seasoning further if required. Bring to a boil and serve.

Liquamen may be approximated in the modern kitchen by boiling over high heat until reduced one-third: 1 ounce of anchovies in olive oil, 1-1/2 cups of water, and 1 teaspoon of oregano. Strain twice through a tea strainer and add 1 ounce of grape juice plus 1/2 teaspoon of salt.

A pungent annual related to mint, sweet basil is the most commonly grown basil today, although there are many others in cultivation. The stem is obtusely quadrangular. Leaves are long and pointed, rich green in color, paler green beneath, opposite, stalked, and softly smooth and cool to the touch. White flowers are in clusters along a spike terminating each leafy branch.

Flourishes best in a rich soil.

Furnishes an aromatic, volatile, camphoraceous oil.

Aromatic and carminative.

BAY

ἡ δάφνη

(daphne)

Laurus

*B*ay is the noble laurel, the tree whose branches the messenger god Hermes struck against a pomegranate stick to invent the art of fire. The laurel became Apollo's tree, the metamorphosis of the pursued Daphne (see page 13). In Homer's *Odyssey* the cave of Polyphemus the Cyclops is found by Odysseus "overhung and shaded by laurels" because Polyphemus is one of Apollo's shepherds. The early Greek poet Hesiod, too, was a common shepherd of Apollo until the Muses gave him a laurel branch and breathed into him a divine voice to celebrate the future and the past.

In the Greek religious tradition winners of the Pythian games at Delphi received wreaths of laurel leaves. The custom was later adopted by Roman generals who wore the crown of bay instead of medals. In one of his odes, the Roman poet Horace looked back in time at the Greek poet Pindar and judged him "worthy of Apollo's bay." Julius Caesar's enemies said he wore such wreaths to excess, but his friends claimed it was to conceal his baldness.

The clean pungency of the bay's leaves was believed to ward off lightning and evil magic, to protect dispatches from emperors and warriors, and to destroy pestilential bacteria. The Romans believed that the laurel was the only plant lightning never struck, and for this reason the emperor Tiberius always wore a laurel wreath during electrical storms. The Romans made Strings of Victory from ropes of laurel leaves, and a messenger carrying a scroll tied with such a string was by law not to be detained but rather to be aided to his destination. Bay became a symbol of protection and marital happiness: it appeared at weddings, adorned gifts, and was taken in powdered form to induce virility. Oil of bay was used extensively by the Romans for massage and to perfume bath water. Pliny recommended that a few protective sprigs of laurel be placed under the pillow at night because the soul left the sleeping body.

Theophrastus classified the bay in his *Enquiry into Plants,* calling it *daphnē,* a name he also applies to several other plants not related to *Laurus;* in his *Characters* he observes an overly sanctimonious fourth-century Athenian who daily puts a bay leaf from the temple in his mouth; and, in his *Concerning Odors,* he notes that the fruit of the bay was used to make perfume.

In his *De agri cultura,* Cato gives recipes for the breads, cheeses, and wines made by the Romans of his time. One of these is for a cheese bread called *libum:*

1 cup dry ricotta or farmer's cheese	6 bay leaves
1/2–1 cup unbleached flour	2 tablespoons honey
1 egg, beaten	

Laurus nobilis Linnaeus. *Lauraceae.*

Mash cheese well with fingers in medium-sized bowl until it forms a smooth, lump-less paste. Add flour, mix well with fingers. Add beaten egg and mix well. Dough will be rather sticky. Divide dough into two equal parts; form two round, flat loaves, each 1/2–inch thick. Place each on three bay leaves on a greased baking sheet. Bake at 400° F. in preheated oven for one hour.

Pliny lists eleven types of laurel in his *Natural History.* For medicinal uses, he notes that its leaves, bark, and berries generate heat. An application of the leaves counteracts the poisons of wasps, hornets, bees, and snakes. The tender leaves pounded and mixed with pearl-barley are good for eye inflammations. The pounded leaves of Delphic bay are to be sniffed to keep away the infection of plague, and they are even more effective if the leaves are also burned.

Apicius suggests that a dressing for roast suckling pig with honey be stirred with a whip of fresh laurel twigs.

Bay trees as well as myrtle and rosemary were traditional plants in Roman gardens. The bay is often depicted in Roman wall paintings, and a carbonized bay tree was found in the outer peristyle of the House of the Faun at Pompeii where it had been growing at the time of the eruption of Vesuvius in A.D. 79.

A small tree with smooth bark, olive-green or reddish, the bay's luxuriant evergreen leaves are alternate with short stalks, lanceolate, thick, smooth, and shining dark green. Flowers are small, yellow, and unisexual, and grow in small clusters.

Ordinary soil conditions.

A greenish-yellow volatile oil contains a high percentage of oxygenated compounds. Berries contain both fixed and volatile oils; the former, known as oil of bays, includes laurostearine, the ester of lauric acid.

Leaves, berries, and oil have excitant and narcotic properties. Leaves are also diaphoretic and in large doses emetic.

BORAGE

τὸ βούγλωσσον

(bouglōsson)

Euphrosinum

*B*orage is native to southern Europe and Asia Minor. Although it has been used since antiquity as both food and drug, the origin of its name is still disputed. Some writers maintain that the Latin *borago,* from which our popular name for the herb derives, is a corruption of *corago*—from *cor,* the heart, and *ago,* I bring—because of the coridal effect of the plant. In all countries bordering the Mediterranean where it still grows abundantly, the name of the herb is spelled with a double "r." Linguists, therefore, say that our borage may derive from the Italian *burra,* or the French *bourra,* meaning hair or wool. Both of these words in turn came from the Latin *burra,* a shaggy garment, which could refer to the thick covering of hair over the entire plant. One writer suggests that its name is derived from the Arabic *abu rach,* father of sweat, because borage was used as a sudorific in antiquity. Another proposes a Celtic derivation, from *barrach,* meaning man of courage, because of the age-old verse, "I, borage, always give courage *(Ego, Borago, gaudia semper ago)."*

The cooling properties of borage were thought to help reduce fever, and a syrup made from its leaves was used to quiet a "lunatic person." Dioscorides calls it *bouglōsson* and Pliny *buglossos,* because its leaf shape and texture are like the tongue of an ox, and Ox-tongue is still one of its common names. Both commented that when the leaves are added to wine it increases the exhilarating effect, and so, reports Pliny, it is also called *euphrosinum,* the plant that cheers.

A hardy annual, rough with white, stiff, prickly hairs, the round stems are branched, hollow, succulent. Leaves alternate, large, wrinkled, deep green, oval, the lower ones stalked, the margins entire but wavy. Flowers are bright blue and star-shaped, distinguished from those of related plants by their prominent blue-black anthers which have been described as their beauty spots.

Flourishes in ordinary soil. If left alone, borage will seed itself freely.

Contains potassium and calcium combined with mineral acids. The fresh juice provides thirty percent, the dried herb three percent of nitrate of potash. Stems and leaves supply much saline mucilage as well as nitre and common salt when boiled. The wholesome, invigorating properties of borage are attributed to these saline qualities.

Diuretic, demulcent, emollient.

Borago officinalis Linnaeus. *Boraginaceae.*

CHAMOMILE

τὸ χαμαίμηλον

(chamaimēlon)

Anthemis

*C*hamomile has been included in the medicine chest of the Mediterranean region for well over 2,000 years, and it continues to be a useful medicinal plant. The herb's generic name derives from the Greek *chamaimēlon,* from *chamai,* "on the ground," and *melon,* "apple," a reference to its distinctive smell when fresh. Chamomile's specific name, *nobile*—noble or noted—may refer to its healing qualities.

Dioscorides calls the herb *anthemis,* from the Greek *anthos,* a flower. He distinguished three kinds of chamomile that differed only in the flower, and recorded the fact that it "grows in rough places and by the way." He also noted that infusions of the roots, flowers, and leaves have a warming effect, adding that the herb relieves upset stomachs, soothes nerves, and is useful in kidney and liver diseases. One variety of chamomile accounts in part for the delightful aroma that fills the air around the Acropolis today.

Pliny notes that *anthemis* was highly praised by the physician Asclepiades. He concurs with Dioscorides on names and types of chamomile and on harvesting it in the spring. It was gathered on thin soils or near foot paths and put aside for making chaplets or garlands. During the same season physicians also pounded the herb's leaves, blossoms, and roots into lozenges. He recommends the pounded herb in one-drachma doses for every kind of snake bite and agrees with Dioscorides on its efficacy for kidney and bladder diseases.

Anthemis chia or Greek chamomile is native to central and eastern Mediterranean areas. *Chamaemelum nobile* or Roman chamomile is native to western Europe, naturalized but not native to Italy, and not found in Greece. *Chamomilla recutita* (L.) Rauschert *[Matricaria recutita* L.*]* or German chamomile, native to most of Europe and known also as sweet or false chamomile, it is an annual species used for the sweet chamomile tea drunk today.

Roman chamomile is a downy, sweet-scented but bitter-tasting perennial. Leaves are feathery and fernlike. Stems branch and creep, rooting as the plant spreads, bearing in summer daisy-like flowers with yellow centers surrounded by white florets. The fruit is small and dry.

Prefers dry, flat area and sandy soil.

Flowers contain a volatile oil, a bitter extractive, and little tannic acid.

Carminative, sedative, and tonic.

Chamaemelum nobile (L.) Allioni *[Anthemis nobilis L.]. Compositae.*

CORIANDER

τὸ κορίανδρον

(koriandron)

Coriandrum

Coriander has been cultivated and used as an aromatic stimulant and a seasoning from very early times. Coriander seeds have been found in Bronze Age ruins on the Aegean islands of Thera and Terasia and in the tombs of the pharaohs. It was used in Mycenae and Cyprus, and Hippocrates and other Greek physicians employed it as one of their standard medicinal herbs. Theophrastus studied and described coriander, recognizing it as a kitchen garden staple. Dioscorides calls it *koriandron,* Pliny *coriandrum.*

Roman legions carried coriander to Britain, and the Romans used it in innumerable ways as both food and drug. Varro writes that it was one of the herbs used as a meat preservative: lightly crushed coriander and caraway seeds in vinegar keep meat through the summer. Plautus tells us that it was used to flavor two bland staples of the early Roman diet, barley porridge and mixed boiled greens. A more sophisticated Roman seasoning mixture of republican and imperial times consisted of wild celery, coriander, mint, onion, pennyroyal, rue, savory, and thyme. Virgil added garlic to this mixture, and Apicius made a coriander-flavored sauce for oysters or other shellfish.

Dioscorides records coriander as a well known herb, with a cooling effect when applied with bread or polenta for erysipelas and creeping ulcers. A small amount of coriander seed in passum wine cures intestinal parasites, but too much disturbs the mind. Pliny lists still more remedies: coriander is drunk or applied as an antidote for the poison bite of a specific snake, the *amphisbaena;* and three grains of coriander seed are swallowed for tertian malaria. Pounded with garlic and taken in neat wine, fresh coriander was believed to be aphrodisiac; and some, he adds, believe it beneficial to place coriander under the pillows before sunrise.

Coriander is double in its morphology, bearing two kinds of leaves and two opposed kinds of flowers. An annual with erect stems, the plant is slender and branched. The lowest leaves are stalked and pinnate, leaflets round or oval, slightly lobed. Pale mauve, almost white flowers grow in short–stalked umbels of five to ten rays. Coriander seeds and leaves are intensely pungent.

Warm, dry, light soil.

Seeds contain about one percent of volatile oil, the active ingredient. They yield about five percent of ash and contain also malic acid, tannin, and some fatty matter.

Stimulant, aromatic, carminative.

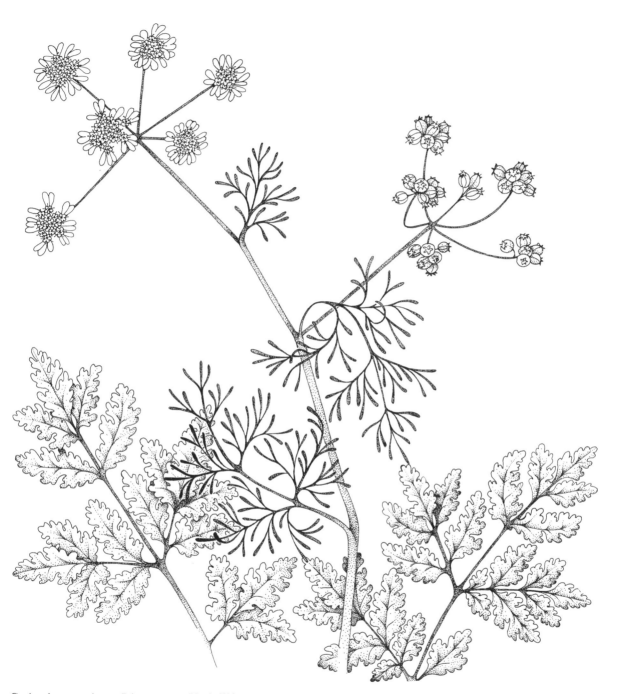

Coriandrum sativum Linnaeus. *Umbelliferae.*

DILL

τὸ ἄνηθον

(anēthon)

Anetum

Dill is native to the Mediterranean and Black Sea regions and it still grows wild in many parts of this area, including the Italian coast. One of the earliest herbs of the ancient world, its use was well established by the time of Aristotle, and Theophrastus analyzed and classified it in terms of its form and growth characteristics, including it in a typical Greek kitchen garden along with the beets and lettuces and onions. Dioscorides and Pliny also knew dill well. Dioscorides calls it the seed of Mercury and refers to it as *anethon* (it is still called *aneth* in some countries). He gives instructions for preparing a medicinal dill oil and prescribes an infusion of dill seed and dried dill leaves for nursing mothers, recommending it too as a carminative, stomachic, diuretic, and hiccough retardant. Too much, he concludes, dulls the sight and promotes impotence.

Pliny recommends dill for much the same illnesses as Dioscorides does. He describes a method for making the cure-all lozenges the Greeks called *theraci*. First, carefully boned and trimmed viper meat is boiled in dill and water. Then the mixture is dried in the shade and shaped into the lozenges used in many different medicines. For hiccoughs he records a remedy of raw cabbage juice in vinegar with dill, coriander, honey, and pepper, adding that wild asparagus water mixed with dill is an aphrodisiac. For barrenness in women he records a cure of the Magi, a group of healers whose magical practices he claims to deplore: the eye of a hyena taken in food with licorice and dill guarantees conception within three days.

The Romans also wore wreaths of dill at their feasts, and dill oil was mixed with the food of gladiators as a tonic. Yet, the word we use for dill comes from the old Norse word *dilla*, which is an allusion to its soothing effect.

Very like its relative fennel, though smaller, dill has feathery leaves with linear, pointed leaflets. Unlike fennel, it seldom has more than a single stalk, and it is an annual. Its stems are smooth and shiny and in midsummer they bear broad, flattened umbels with many small yellow flowers, their tiny petals rolled inward. Flat fruits, commonly known as "seeds," are produced in large quantities. The entire plant is aromatic.

Rich, sandy, well-drained soil.

Dill seed produces a volatile oil composed of a paraffin hydrocarbon and 40–60% of d–carvone with d–limonene.

Stimulant, aromatic, carminative, and stomachic.

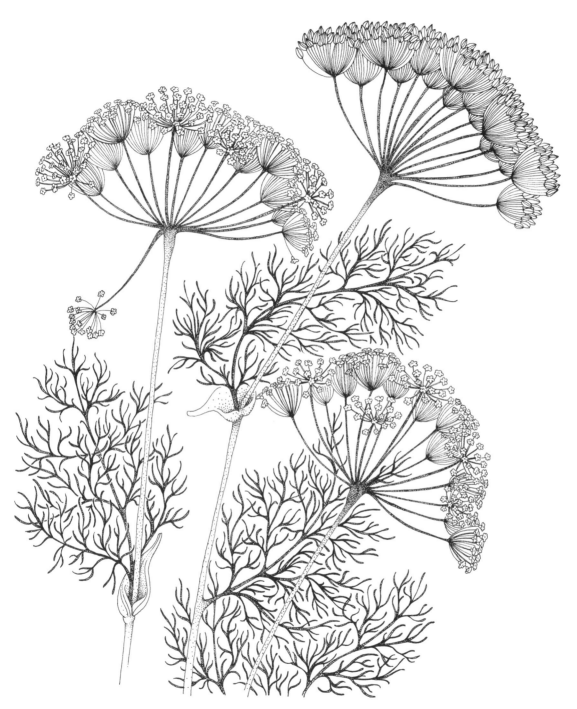

Anethum graveolens Linnaeus. *Umbelliferae.*

FENNEL

τὸ μάραθον

(marathon)

Feniculum

*F*ennel has a history as old as the Mediterranean basin where it originated. The ancient Egyptians, Greeks, and Romans all ate its aromatic fruits and tender shoots. In the midsummer festival Adonia, of ancient times, fennel was among those seeds planted in the rites. A lover of the goddess Aphrodite, Adonis was the beautiful youth whose death and resurrection the festival observed. Around his image fast-germinating plants such as fennel, lettuce, and barley were sown in clay pots. The seeds sprouted quickly and then the sprouts withered from sun and drought. When the plants died, the pots were thrown in the river with images of Adonis. These rites, intended to invoke abundant rainfall in the coming season, may have encouraged pot-culture as a convenient way of growing plants indoors.

Early Greek athletes, in training for the games, ate fennel seeds as a healthful food that also controlled their weight. Theophrastus distinguished two types of *ferula,* calling fennel a *ferula*-like plant. He commented that the two were alike except in size, naming the very tall plant *narthex* and the smaller one *narthekia. Narthex* appears in one of the earliest Greek myths. Prometheus, in a contest with Zeus, stole the glowing charcoal that was fire, carrying it as a gift to mankind in the hollow stalk of the giant fennel plant *(Ferula communis).* Dioscorides distinguished several types, calling one of them *narthex (Ferula communis)* and another *marathon (Foeniculum vulgare).* Herodotus and Ovid both comment that the site of the famous battle of Marathon in eastern Attica was a plain overgrown with fennel. Both *narthex* and *marathon* had medicinal properties, but the juice of *marathon* stalks and leaves was believed to be effective for improving eyesight. Possibly a connection was made with a story Pliny reports: after serpents shed their skins, they rub against the fennel plant to sharpen their eyesight. He attributes twenty-two medicinal remedies to fennel and also distinguishes several different types.

Certainly the Romans delighted in the flavor of fennel. Cato the Elder gives a recipe for curing green olives and then seasoning them with oil, vinegar, salt, fennel, and mastic. His recipe for an olive relish is prepared as follows: remove stones from green, ripe, and mottled olives; chop flesh and add oil, vinegar, fennel, cumin, coriander, mint, and rue; serve in an earthen dish. Young fennel shoots were cooked as vegetables, raw stalks made into salads, and seeds placed under loaves of bread as it was baked to add flavor. Columella gives another recipe, for preserving fennel stems in brine and vinegar. Roman soldiers mixed fennel seed with their meals to assure fighting strength and courage.

Foeniculum vulgare Miller. *Umbelliferae.*

The Apician cookbook contains a recipe for *Tisana taricha,* an herbal barley soup that includes both fresh fennel and fennel seed:

> Soak dried chick peas, lentils, and split peas. Crush barley and boil with the dried vegetables. When cooked add olive oil to taste and chopped leeks, coriander, fresh fennel, dill, beet, mallow, and tender cabbage leaves. Pound a generous quantity of fennel seed, oregano, asafoetida, and lovage; moisten with *liquamen* (see page 29) and add to soup. Serve with finely chopped cabbage leaves on top.

A graceful hardy perennial with shining, cylindrical, blue-green stems. Leaves are bright green and finely feathered. Flowers are bright yellow in large flat umbels. Florence fennel *(F. vulgare* var. *dulce),* also called *finocchio,* has an enlarged leaf base and is used as a vegetable. Young stems of Sicilian fennel *(F. vulgare* var. *piperitum)* can be blanched and eaten like celery.

Full sun and ordinary soil.

Volatile oil of fennel has properties similar to that of dill. The best varieties of fennel yield from 4% to 5% of volatile oil, its principal constituents anethol and fenchone.

Aromatic, carminative, stimulant, stomachic.

GARLIC

τὸ σκόροδον

(skorodon)

Alium

Garlic is of such antiquity that it is difficult to trace its country of origin. Probably from Central Asia, it has been a food and medicinal herb in Europe, Africa, and Asia Minor from earliest times. Plautus, Horace, and Sidonius Apollonaris hated its strong smell, but Hippocrates, Theophrastus, Aristophanes, Virgil, Pliny, and Dioscorides loved it. Odysseus, according to Homer, used *moly* (possibly *Allium nigrum,* a plant with a black root and a milk-white flower) as a charm to prevent the sorceress Circe from turning him into a pig. Theophrastus comments that the superstitious Greek who placed wreaths of garlic on crossroads altars to the goddess Hecate, also purified himself by carrying around a squill or a puppy-dog. It was customary in Greece to deny entrance to the temples of Cybele to anyone who had eaten garlic. Women who attended the Athenian festivals of Thesmorphia and Skira believed that chewing garlic would help them to achieve temporary chastity and increase fertility after a period of abstention. The use of garlic in ritual abstention from sexual relations was part of several ancient ceremonies. Pliny, however, writes that garlic mixed with wine and coriander was a potent aphrodisiac.

Both the Greeks and the Romans consumed garlic in great quantities. Virgil observes in his *Eclogues* that "Thestylus is bruising garlic and wild thyme, strong-smelling herbs for the mowers wearied with the fierce heat." For Horace the smell of garlic was a sign of vulgarity. He found it "more poisonous than hemlock," and he relates that he was made ill by eating it at the table of his wealthy patron Maecenas. Garlic in Rome was dedicated to Mars, the god of war. The Roman legions propagated the plant in conquered lands, believing that if eaten in quantity it would make them courageous in the battlefield.

Aristotle found garlic to be hot, laxative, a cure for hydrophobia and a tonic, but bad for the eyes. Theophrastus observed that there were several kinds of garlic and that it should be planted a little before or after the solstice, when it divides into cloves. The Cyprian excelled in size, he noted, and was not cooked but used in salads, and "when pounded increases wondrously in bulk and makes a foaming dressing." Menander advised—perhaps tongue-in-cheek—that after eating garlic the breath could be neutralized by eating a roasted beet.

Garlic was used throughout antiquity as an antiseptic protection against the plague as well as a powerful charm against the evil eye. (As recently as World War I, garlic used as an antiseptic for wounds saved thousands of lives.)

Allium sativum Linnaeus. *Liliaceae.*

According to Pliny, garlic and onion were invoked as gods by the Egyptians when they took oaths. Pliny saw garlic as an herbal remedy with powerful properties: to keep off the serpents and scorpions, to cure bites, to relieve asthma, toothaches, sprains and ruptures, and to induce sleep. Pliny reports that the objectionable smell of garlic can be prevented if it is planted when the moon is below the horizon and gathered when it is in conjunction. Dioscorides concurs with Pliny on garlic's effectiveness and Galen eulogizes it as a rustic *theriac*, or cure-all.

Sala cattabia, an Apician recipe for a filled loaf of bread cooled in snow, reveals its rural origin in the use of garlic:

A one-pound loaf of unsliced bread, round, rectangular, or baguette

3 tablespoons white vinegar ⎤
1 ounce cold water ⎬ to coat inside of loaf
1/2 teaspoon ground cumin ⎦

2 chicken breasts or 1/2 chicken ⎤ cooked in additional olive oil
3 chicken livers (optional) ⎦

1 cucumber, peeled, thinly sliced	1/4 cup honey
4 ounces dry ricotta or feta	2 teaspoons mint
1/4 cup pine nuts	2 cloves garlic, finely minced
1 teaspoon capers	2 coriander leaves
1 ounce onion, finely chopped	3 ounces olive oil
1/4 teaspoon ground pepper	

Prepare bread loaf as a "box" with detachable cover, leaving the walls and the cover about 1/2-inch thick; brush the insides with the vinegar-cold water-cumin mixture. Fill the box with layers of the remaining ingredients. Replace the cover. Chill in refrigerator or snow for one hour. Slice and serve.

Garlic is a perennial with long, narrow, flat leaves that grow up from the bulb. The bulb is of a compound nature, consisting of numerous bulblets, known as "cloves," grouped together between membraneous scales and enclosed in a white skin. White flowers at the end of a stalk rising directly from the bulb are grouped together in an umbel and among them are small bulbils with a bract below.

Soil may be sandy, loam, or clay, though rich, moist, sandy soil is best.

Active properties of garlic depend on a pungent, volatile, essential oil. The penetrating odor of this herb is due to the intensely smelling sulphuret of allyl, so diffusive that even when the bulb is applied to the soles of the feet, its odor is exhaled by the lungs.

Diaphoretic, diuretic, expectorant, stimulant.

IRIS

ἡ ἶρις

(iris)

Iris

*T*he genus *Iris* was named for the Greek messenger goddess who personified the rainbow connecting heaven and earth. The special messenger of Zeus and Hera, Iris first appears in Homer's *Iliad.* Both the Egyptians and the Greeks cultivated the iris and admired its elegant beauty. As a symbol of power and majesty, the iris was also dedicated to Juno.

Theophrastus, Dioscorides, and Pliny were well acquainted with the iris and its product, orrisroot. Orrisroot was used in medicines, cosmetics, and perfumes. Macedonia, Elis, and Corinth were famous for their unguents of iris, and Dioscorides and Pliny both remark that the best orrisroot is Illyrian. Most of the irises grown by the Greeks and Romans belonged to a complex of natural hybrids taken into gardens at a very early time for their medicinal value and their fragrance. Extremely persistent, many of these ancient iris cultivars have been grown in gardens ever since.

Iris is the first plant on Dioscorides' list of aromatics, and his descriptions fit several of the *Iris X germanica* natural hybrids cultivated in ancient gardens of Asia Minor, the Balkans, and Italy. "Iris," he writes, "is so named from its resemblance to the rainbow in heaven, but it bears leaves like a little sword... the flowers on the stalk bend in, one over another... they are either white *(I. albicans)* or pale *(I. X germanica 'Florentina')* or black *(I. X germanica)* or purple *(I. aphylla)* or azure *(I. pallida).* The roots are knotty, of a sweet savor and after wilting should be dried in the shade."

Pliny remarks that the iris like many other exquisitely perfumed flowers cannot be made into garlands, but that its valuable root yields numerous unguents and medicines. Orrisroot is useful tied to teething or coughing babies, injected for tapeworm, or chewed to sweeten foul breath.

Iris X germanica and its off-white "Florentine" form are robust perennials with sword-like, blue-green leaves. Large blue, purple, or lavender–white flowers have bright yellow beards on the bending petals, or falls.

The characteristic violet odor of the root develops gradually after drying. The chief constituent of orrisroot, oil of orris, contains about 85% of odorless myristic acid. The violet-like fragrance comes from a liquid ketone named irone.

Rarely used in medicine today, orrisroot is now used in perfume, as a fixative, in sachets and dusting powders, as an absorbent in dry shampoos, in dentifrices, and in pastilles.

Iris X germanica 'Florentina'. Iridaceae.

MINT

Mint was prized by the Greeks and Romans for both its medicinal value and its refreshing fragrance. Ovid has the hospitable Baucis and Philemonon scour their table with fresh mint (probably *Mentha aquatica,* or Water Mint) before setting out food for the gods Zeus and Hermes. An origin for mint is told in a late Greek myth about Hades' pursuit of the nymph Minthē, who is changed into a mint plant by his jealous wife, Persephone. Mint, rosemary, and myrtle were used in ancient funeral rites to offset the smell of decay. *Mentha pulegium* (Pennyroyal) was used in a barley water beverage drunk by ancient Greek harvesters and was an active ingredient in a similar draught, *kykeon,* drunk by the goddess Demeter and offered to the initiates at her mysterious rites in the temple at Eleusis (see page 9).

Greeks and Romans used mint (probably *M. aquatica* or *M. pulegium*) to scent their bath water and as a restorative from fainting. In Athens each part of the body was perfumed with a different scent—Greek gods were always "sweet-smelling" or "fragrant"—and mint was used specifically on the arms. *Mentha pulegium* was twisted into wreaths for Greek brides because of its long, flexible stems, its profuse blossoms, and its festive aroma. It is also the species the followers of Bacchus wore to dispel the effects of wine. Varro advised that a garland of this mint was better for the bedroom than a garland of roses. *Pulegium* derives from the Greek *pulex* meaning flea, and because of the power of this mint to keep these pests away, it was strewn on dining room floors in an age when food scraps were tossed under the table for dogs. Pliny recommends mint for stuffing cushions and remarks on its pervasive scent at country banquets (probably *M. pulegium* and *M. aquatica*).

Just the smell of mint, says Pliny, refreshes our spirits and gives zest to food. Both Greeks and Romans wore mint as banquet wreaths, used it as table sprays, and added it to their sauces and wines (probably *Mentha spicata,* or Spearmint).

Deriving from its mythological origin, the generic name *Mentha* first was given to mint by Theophrastus (Greek *minthē*). Aristotle and others forbade the use of mint by soldiers because it was thought to lessen or destroy their aggressiveness. Earlier, mint was part of Hippocrates' *materia medica,* but he believed too much mint could cause impotence. Both Dioscorides and Pliny wrote of the many virtues of mint, and each distinguished several wild and cultivated species. Wild mint *(mentastrum,* probably *Mentha aquatica)* transplanted from the mountains, says Pliny, grows on the walls of wells and around fishponds. Mint cures forty-one ailments, and pennyroyal cures another twenty-five. Mint prevents milk from curdling and thus is added to milk for drinking. It cures

Mentha aquatica Linnaeus; *M. spicata* L; *M. pulegium* L. *Labiatae.*

sores, spasms, lung complaints, hiccoughs, iliac trouble, headache, eye infections, and it prevents chafing even if only held in the hand. Sprays of pennyroyal or mint revive one from a faint. Applications of pennyroyal cure headaches, and its very smell protects the head against injury from heat, cold, or thirst. Two sprays of pennyroyal tucked behind the ears prevent the harmful effect of heat. If unhealthful water must be drunk, it can be made safe by sprinkling pounded pennyroyal on it. Wild mint chewed or applied cures elephantiasis, a chance discovery at the time of Pompeius Magnus by a victim of the disease who smeared his face for shame. Its leaves applied or drunk in wine cure serpent bites; leaves dried to a powder are kept as an antidote for all poisons. Mint prevents amorous dreams. For dandruff, pour minted vinegar over the head in the sun.

Dioscorides' herbal includes six varieties of mint. The Roman *mentha* he calls *edysmos emeros* (probably *Mentha spicata*), and he ascribes to it properties that stop bleeding, kill roundworms, and provoke lust. Rubbed on a rough tongue, this mint makes it smooth. It is good for the stomach and fit for sauces. Some people, he adds, call pennyroyal *blechon,* because when cattle eat its flowers they bleat.

Mints are a fairly small group of hardy, aromatic, square-stemmed perennials, difficult to classify because many natural hybrids occur and intermediate forms are common. The current edition of *Flora of Europe* lists seven species of mint native to Italy, including *M. pulegium* (which does not hybridize with the rest), *M. aquatica,* and *M. spicata* (Spearmint or Yerba Buena). Spearmints present a complex problem, as they are not known to be native anywhere. Hybrids, they arose in cultivation and are normally sterile. Peppermint *(M. X piperita)* adds a further complication. A hybrid of *M. aquatica* and *M. spicata,* if present in ancient Greece and Rome, would have been strictly limited to the garden and perhaps passed from one druggist or gourmet to another. Six of these seven mint species plus an untold number of their hybrids grew wild in the Mediterranean area, further complicating the problem of exactly identifying those mints referred to by classical authors.

Moist situation preferred but mint will succeed in almost any soil.

All the mints yield fragrant oils by distillation. Peppermint oil ranks first among essential oils. Menthol is its chief constituent, and that of spearmint oil is carvone.

Stimulant, carminative, antispasmodic.

MUSTARD

Mustard, Pliny tells us, was judged by Pythagoras to be the most important of the pungent herbs since no other penetrates as far into the nostrils and the brain. White mustard, *Brassica hirta,* of the cabbage genus, appears in Theophrastus, Dioscorides, and Pliny, although they all used the Greek word for mustard, *sinapi.* Mustard was so important to physicians in antiquity that they attributed its discovery to Asclepius, the god of medicine.

Mustard sows itself so easily that the Greeks and Romans could either cultivate it or gather it wild. Great mustard eaters, the Romans used it simply and directly, seasoning their meat as they chewed it by putting a few seeds into their mouths. They also pounded and steeped it in new wine, and probably introduced the plant to Britain. Mustard leaves were eaten by the Greeks and the Romans as a vegetable, but the dramatist Plautus (254?-184 B.C.), a fussy eater, disapproved of this use. In his *Pseudolus,* a satire on Roman cuisine, a cook complains of other cooks who season "herbs with other herbs" by describing a dish of mixed greens—coriander, fennel, garlic, Macedonian parsley, sorrel, cabbage, white beets, and chard seasoned with expensive *silphium* and ubiquitous ground mustard. The last ingredient Plautus termed "a frightful poison which when crushed makes the eyes water." Pliny, on the other hand, later remarked that mustard leaves improve the taste of other plants cooked in the same pot.

Hippocrates advocates the use of white mustard seed, taken internally or applied as a counter-irritating poultice made with vinegar. Dioscorides recommends mustard plants that are new and in their prime: "Choose that which is not very dry and very red or full, but...when broken looks green inside and juicy." In general, he says, it is good for any internal pain of long duration and it cures by drawing out from deep within. Mustard juice mixed with honey and water (hydromel) and gargled is good for inflamed tonsils. As an ointment it cures dandruff and clears the complexion. Beaten with figs, it improves hearing and alleviates noise in the ears, and mustard juice in honey improves the eyesight.

Pliny claims that pungent, fiery mustard was found effective for forty-four different ailments, coinciding with some of those noted by Dioscorides. Pounded and applied with vinegar, it relieves serpent bites and scorpion stings; it counteracts fungus poisoning; chewed, it alleviates toothache; it is beneficial for all stomach troubles; pounded with equal parts of figs and cumin and applied externally, it is good for dropsy; its powerful smell when mixed with vinegar revives those in epileptic fits, faints, or melancholic states. He notes, too, that mustard seeds germinate quickly—in four days—and that they should be planted at the autumn equinox along with coriander, dill, sorrel, and chervil. While it grows entirely wild, he adds, it is improved by being transplanted.

Many kinds of salads were included in the Roman cuisine. Pliny reports that turnips are stained six different colors—although purple is the only one suitable for the table. He adds that while turnips are popular with several kinds of dressings, when subdued by the pungency of mustard they make an unbeatable salad.

Among the fish sauces in the Apician cookbook is *Ius in locusta et cammaris:*

> Sauté a chopped scallion and add pepper, lovage, cumin, Jericho dates, honey, vinegar, wine, *liquamen* (see page 29), oil, and *defrutum* (must or grape juice). Add mustard and serve with steamed shellfish.

Mustard is an erect annual with pinnatifid leaves; its four yellow petals, arranged in the form of a cross, alternate with the four sepals. Even when powdered, the mustard seed is odorless; it becomes pungent only when the powder is moistened with water, causing the formation of the volatile oil of mustard.

Dry soil and direct sun.

Epidermal cells of the seed coat of white mustard contain mucilage, and cotyledons have 23–26% of a fixed oil of glycerides of oleic, stearic, and erucic or brassic acids.

Irritant, stimulant, diuretic, emetic.

Brassica hirta Moench *[Sinapis alba* L.*]. Cruciferae.*

MYRTLE

ἡ μύρτος

(myrtos)

Myrtus

*M*yrtle is the sacred plant of the Greek goddess Aphrodite and the Roman goddess Venus, and the messenger god Hermes fashioned his magical sandals of myrtle branches. Fragrant myrtle is associated with both love and death in the ancient world. The myrtle was originally a death-tree, on which Hippolytus in flight from Athens caught his chariot reins and was dragged to death by his horses. A myrtle was reported to have grown near his hero's shrine. The Myrtle-nymphs were prophetesses who taught the god Aristaeus, son of Apollo and Cyrene, the useful arts of making cheese, building beehives, and cultivating olives. Venus, a very early Latin goddess of spring, seems to have been first called Murcia, a deity that later was interpreted as Myrtea, goddess of myrtles.

Sacred myrtle grew in the groves at Eleusis when the initiates to the religious mysteries strolled there, wearing the leaves as wreaths. Myrtle, along with mint and rosemary, was burned from very early times in funeral rites. Theophrastus, however, in his *Characters,* written in the later fourth century B.C., chides those superstitious Greeks who on the fourth and seventh days of each month buy myrtle boughs to garland their household gods. In the first century, Pliny reports a belief that on an extended journey a foot traveller who carries a myrtle stick or rod will never feel weariness or tedium.

In his *Enquiry into Plants,* Theophrastus tells us that of all cultivated plants myrtle and bay are least likely to thrive in cold regions. Especially myrtle, he adds, for on Mount Olympus bay is abundant, but there is no myrtle; yet in the Propontis, myrtle and bay are both found on the mountains. In *Concerning Odors* he records a myrtle perfume made from the leaves and fruit of the tree. Athenians regarded the berries of the myrtle as a confection. A fragment from Antiphanes' (480–334 B.C.) comedy the *Cretans* begins: "But first of all/I want some myrtle berries on the table/which I may eat just as it pleases me/And they must be Phibalean, very fine/Fit for a garland." Pliny notes that even when chewed the day before, they make the mouth smell sweet and that the women eat them in Menander's comedy *Synaristosae* (Women at Lunch). His final word on the subject is a "prescription for offensive breath, a very embarrassing complaint. Myrtle leaves with an equal weight of *lentisci* (a Syrian nut) and one-half quantity of old wine may be chewed with benefit in the morning."

In his *De agri cultura* Cato gives instructions for making myrtle wine: dry black myrtle berries in the shade; when shrivelled, store until vintage time; crush one-half peck of myrtle berries in three gallons of must; seal the vessel; when fermentation stops, remove the myrtle berries.

Myrtus communis Linnaeus. *Myrtaceae.*

In the *Aeneid,* Virgil portrays Augustus encircling his temples with ancestress' myrtle to show his descent from the goddess Venus. He moves then to the "shores rejoicing in myrtle groves," "the myrtle in stout spear shafts," and again later to "the shore-loving myrtle." Horace encircled his brow often, preferring simpler myrtle to the more fashionable garlands of Persian roses, as he stretched out to sip wine or to make love under the moon on his Sabine farm: "Cytherean Venus already leads her bands of dancers beneath the overhanging moon... Now is the fitting time to bind our glistening locks with green myrtle."

Dioscorides calls the myrtle *myrsine* and distinguishes a black and a white variety. He considers the black better medicinally and lists dozens of remedies made from it. The fruit is good for hemoptysis and ulcers, as is the juice of green myrtle which also helps the stomach. A decoction of the fruit dyes the hair black, and mixed with wine it cures obstinate sores of the body extremities. Applied with flour, it relieves eye inflammations. Pliny independently lists similar uses and adds a few others. Oil from the same myrtle is milder than the juice, and so also is myrtle wine which never intoxicates. A decoction of leaves in wine clears up freckles, hangnails, whitlows, sores of the eyelid, and venereal diseases in men. For swelling of the groin, one need merely carry a sprig of myrtle that has touched neither iron nor the ground. Pliny also refers to a wild myrtle ("myrtus silvestris"), which can be distinguished from the cultivated by its red berries and small size, and young stalks cooked in ashes are eaten like asparagus. The plant that was eaten has been identified by modern botanists as *Ruscus aculeatus,* commonly known as Butcher's Broom or Jew's Myrtle.

Full sun and ordinary soil.

A strongly scented evergreen shrub with glossy bright green leaves, white sweet-scented flowers, and blue-black or creamy white berries. Bark, leaves, flowers, and fruit are all aromatic.

ONION

τὸ κρόμμυον

(krommyon)

Cepa

*O*nions belong to the lily family, and while there is no archaeological proof of the onion in ancient Greece, linguistic evidence suggests that the other well known members of the genus *Allium*—leeks and garlic—go back to the Early Bronze Age. The wise Nestor brought bread and onion and wine to cure the wounded physician Machaon in Homer's *Iliad,* and several hundred years later the onion was still a basic food and medicine in both Greece and Rome, especially for the poor. By about 500 B.C., quantities of onions were produced in Attica with other basic vegetables such as cabbage, garlic, lentils, and peas.

Allium appears in Hippocrates' *materia medica,* and Theophrastus was acquainted with several varieties of onion that undoubtedly were used by the Greeks. Theophrastus distinguished Sardinian, Chidian, and Samothracian onions: annual, divided (shallot), and Ascalonian. All are planted, he advises, after the rising of Arcturus, while the earth is still warm, so that the rain may water them. The Greek playwright Eubulus (active about 370 B.C.), in a parody of the earlier tragedians, portrays a carnivorous Heracles demanding plenty of boiled beef and roast pig:

> But I have not come here to fill myself
> With cabbages, or benjamin, or other
> Impious and bitter dainties, or with onions.

Nero is said to have favored leeks to strengthen his voice before making speeches, and onions were on Horace's list of economical foods. Apicius used onions, leeks, shallots, chives, and sometimes garlic in his sauces, dressings, and vegetables. One distinctive Apician dish, *Pisa farsilis,* was served on a silver platter, with a subtle white sauce:

1 cup split peas	4 tablespoons pine nuts
1 tablespoon olive oil	1 tablespoon ginger
4 leeks	1 tablespoon oregano
1 small cube salt pork	1 tablespoon lovage
2 coriander leaves	1/4 teaspoon pepper
1/4 pound pork ⎤	1 teaspoon cornstarch
1 chicken breast ⎥ cooked	*Liquamen*
4 pork sausages ⎥ and chopped	
1 brain ⎦	

Boil peas until tender; add oil and set aside. Cook leeks with salt pork, coriander, and *liquamen* (see page 29). Moisten pounded ginger, oregano, lovage, pepper with leek stock; thicken with cornstarch, and add to leeks. Line a mold with sausage casings (or oiled wax paper), covering bottom with pine nuts and some of the peas; next arrange layers of pork, leeks, chicken, sausage, brain, peas, ending with a layer of peas. Bake in a 350° F. oven for one hour. For sauce, blend two hard-boiled egg whites with 1/2 teaspoon white pepper, one tablespoon each of pine nuts and honey, 1/4 cup white wine, and *liquamen* to taste. Bring to a boil and pour over unmolded peas.

Dioscorides' herbal has an extended entry on the onion. He calls it *kromuon* and describes it as biting, appetite- and thirst–provoking, attenuating, nauseating, and purging. Onion clears the head through the nostrils, and onion juice mixed with honey improves dull eyesight. Pounded with salt, rue, and honey, it cures dog bites. Mixed with poultry grease it is good for the stomach, for hearing difficulties, noise in the ears, and ear infections. Rubbed on the head, it is good for baldness. Too much onion causes headaches, and it produces somnolence in the sick. Dioscorides is even more cautious: leek juice dulls the eyesight and causes troublesome dreams. Mixed with vinegar and manna, however, the juice stops bleeding, especially nosebleeds. Two drachmas of leek seed drunk with an equal quantity of myrtle berries stops recurrent spitting of blood.

In Egypt, says Pliny, people swear by the onion and garlic as if they were deities. Juvenal (60?–140) also supports this story, but it would appear that a large consumption of onions as food by Egyptian laborers is closer to fact. Pliny lists a number of onion varieties according to their pungency: onions from Africa, Gaul, Tusculum, Ascalon, and Amiternae. There are no wild onions, says Pliny. Cultivated onions, to which he ascribes twenty-seven cures, improve dim vision because the mere smell causes the nose to run, although an even better cure is onion juice applied to the eye. Onions induce sleep; chewed with bread they heal mouth sores; applied in vinegar they heal abrasions. Yet, he adds, there are remarkable differences of opinion on onions among physicians—the latest ones hold that they are injurious to the viscera and the digestion. The school of the physician Asclepiades (first century B.C.) holds that onions promote a clear complexion and eaten daily on an empty stomach they preserve good health. Pliny reports that leeks counteract mushroom poisoning, heal wounds, are aphrodisiac, quench thirst, and dispel hangovers. Leeks also impart brilliance to the voice.

Raw onion seems to have been scorned by some in Rome, but the ordinary Roman traditionally ate a breakfast of bread and onion. Columella highly recommended the onions of Pompeii. Yet, onion vendors there were kept out of the fruit and vegetable sellers' guild and had to organize independently.

The onion is a hardy perennial with succulent hollow stems, crowned by a head of blossoms sometimes mixed with bulblets. In the Egyptian onion the weight of the bulblets drops the whole stem to the ground, where the bulbs take root and form another colony; normal *Allium cepa* reproduces from seed.

Full sun in well-cultivated and drained, fertile garden soil.

Antiseptic, diuretic.

Allium cepa Linnaeus. *Liliaceae.*

OREGANO

*O*regano is called wild marjoram, *agrioriganos,* or *Origanum vulgare.* The word *origanum* derives from two Greek words, *oros,* meaning mountain, and *ganos,* joy. The joyous mountains—the hillsides of ancient Greece—in summer would have been soft pink and white with flowering oregano.

Oregano was customarily planted on graves in ancient Greece, and if it flowered the dead person was thought to be ensured a happy after-life. Theophrastus writes that an oregano growing on Crete, *Origanum dictamnus* (Dittany of Crete) is favored by goats, and "the story of the arrows is also said to be true—that if goats eat it when they have been shot, it rids them of the arrows." Dioscorides distinguishes several varieties, reflecting some of the confusion about oregano and marjoram that persists today. Yet for Dioscorides each variety had medicinal properties; although most effective are the leaves of *sampsychon (Origanum majorana* or Sweet Marjoram), which are also made into crowns; the leaves and flowers of *agrioriganos (Origanum vulgare),* drunk with wine for snake bite; and *origanos (Origanum heracleoticum,* said to have been discovered by Heracles) for earache, enlarged tonsils and uvula, convulsions, dropsy, and narcotic poisoning. He describes *dictamnon* (Dittany of Crete) as an herb like pennyroyal but with larger, downy leaves, and a stronger medicinal action. "Such is the force of this herb that even when smelled it drives away—and touched it kills—poisonous beasts."

Pliny, too, distinguishes several varieties, and suggests adding oregano and cress to wine for asthma and coughs. *Origanum heracleoticum* mixed with salt he recommends for the eyes, and mixed into a broth with meal, oil, and vinegar for coughs, liver complaints, pain in the side, and especially for snake bite. Pliny also refers to the use of two different kinds of oregano for making garlands, one with no seeds, and the other, called Cretan, with a perfume. Athenaeus disapproves of marjoram garlands because they excite the nerves.

A hardy perennial with creeping roots and often purple stems. Leaves are opposite, gray-green, and elliptical in cultivated forms. Flowers in spikes are pink, white, or pale purple. *Origanum vulgare, O. onites, O. majorana,* and *O. heracleoticum* are the species most often used as seasoning.

Full sun and average garden soil, on the dry side, and always well drained.

Yields about two percent of a volatile oil, separated by distillation. Not to be confused with oil of origanum, which is extracted from thyme.

Stimulant, carminative, diaphoretic, and mildly tonic.

Origanum vulgare Linnaeus. *Labiatae.*

PARSLEY

τὸ σέλινον

(selinon)

Petroselinum

*P*arsley has a history of intriguing contradictions. Native to Sardinia, according to Linnaeus, parsley probably originated in the eastern Mediterranean or in Asia Minor. Dedicated to Persephone, Queen of Hades and symbol of spring, it was believed by the ancient Greeks to visit the underworld nine times before sprouting. Parsley wreaths were placed on the tombs of the dead and awarded to the victors of the Nemean games—a survival of funeral games on the death of an important person. Because of its sacred association with oblivion and death, parsley was never brought to the table in early Greece, and there was a superstition about transplanting young parsley.

About 270 B.C. the Greek poet Theocritus wrote of parsley garlands worn at a royal wedding:

> At Sparta's palace, twenty beautiful maids
> the pride of Greece, fresh garlands
> > crowned their heads
> With hyacinths and twining parsley dressed,
> Graced joyful Menelaus' marriage feast.

Theophrastus identified *oreoselinon* (Mountain Parsley) and distinguished both a smooth and a curly variety in his *Enquiry into Plants*. "*Oreoselinon,*" says Dioscorides, "some call *petroselinum sylvestre*…It grows in rocky places." *Petroselinum* refers to its natural habitat and derives from the Greek *petros* meaning rock or stone, and *selinon,* the Greek name for wild parsley.

Plautus hated parsley, but Pliny tells us that it was a universal favorite in first-century Rome. Everywhere in the country sprigs of it could be found swimming in draughts of milk. In sauces it enjoyed a unique popularity. Good for the eyes if applied with honey, fresh parsley was thrown into ponds to cure sickly fish. Pliny admits that no other plant had caused such controversy: the physician–botanists Chrysippus and Dionysus agree that eating parsley is a sin, because it honors the dead at funeral feasts; they also find it bad for the eyesight and a cause of barrenness. Cooks used parsley to remove the tang of vinegar from food, and butlers used bags of parsley to rid wine of bad odors. The Romans often ate parsley on bread for breakfast. Worn in garlands around the neck at banquets, parsley absorbed the fumes of wine.

A hardy biennial, usually cultivated as an annual. Leaves are bright green, divided, and in some varieties tightly curled.

Ordinary, well-worked, moist soil, partially shaded.

Seeds contain an oil of terpenes and apiol.

Diuretic, carminative, tonic.

Petroselinum crispum Miller. *Umbelliferae*.

ROSE

τὸ ῥόδον
(rhodon)
Rosa

*R*oses grow over much of the northern hemisphere, and the first rose preceded the first man. The earliest-known fossil imprint of a sprig of rose leaves found in Colorado is considered 40,000,000 years old, and the oldest known depiction of a rose is in the Blue Bird fresco, a Bronze Age wall painting from the Palace of Knossos in Crete. While this rose is usually described as six-petalled by modern writers, it originally had only five petals—the sixth is a restorer's error. In the *Iliad* Homer observes the "rosy-fingered Dawn" and as Hector lay dead outside the gates of Troy his wife Andromache, unaware of her loss, "wove upon her loom, deep in the lofty house, a double purple web with rose design." Sappho of Lesbos, about 600 B.C., sang of the rose in several of her lyric poems. Later, Herodotus reported that magnificent sixty-petalled roses grew in the "Gardens of Midas" in Macedon, and Theophrastus referred to a hundred-petalled rose. Both roses were probably forms of the Damask Rose.

Greek myth and legend identified the rose most closely with Aphrodite, the goddess of love, and in Rome it became the flower of Venus. Greek *rhodon,* Latin *rosa,* meaning red, refers to the deep rose-pink well known to the ancients. Its color probably gave rise to the myth of Aphrodite and her lover Adonis from whose blood the rose grew. Early in its history, the Greek island of Rhodes made the flower its symbol, and coins with rose images were used as currency across the Mediterranean from archaic times until Rhodes was conquered by the Romans in the first century B.C. (see page 14).

The Mediterranean area probably once blossomed with wild roses. Among them was the *Rosa gallica,* an ancestor of most modern roses. The rose had already been transformed from single to double before 300 B.C., when Theophrastus described the many different roses he knew, roses of from five to one hundred petals. Most of those roses called "hundred-petalled," he says, grow in profusion on Mount Pangaeus near Philippi where the townspeople obtain them for transplanting.

Dioscorides gives recipes for rose salves and liquids for the eyes, ears, gums, and intestines; as wound antidotes; and as eye makeup. *Rhodides,* little pomanders made of rose petals, Indian nard, and myrrh are worn "around women's necks instead of necklaces, dulling the unsavory smell of sweat." Dioscorides does not connect *rhodon* with another herb that he calls *kynosbaton,* a shrub "much greater than a common bush, almost as big as a tree, with leaves larger than the myrtle but strong thorns on the branches; a white flower; a fruit somewhat like an olive pit that grows red when ripe and is downy inside." While the Greeks did not recognize this plant as a rose, it clearly fits the description of *Rosa canina,* the Dog Rose or Dogberry. Its fruit, or hips, as other

Rosa canina Linnaeus; *R. X damascena; R. gallica 'Officinalis.'* Rosaceae.

parts of the rose plant, were assigned specific medicinal uses by Theophrastus, Dioscorides, and Pliny.

Pliny watches a rose open: "Every bud appears at first enclosed in a shell full of grains, which presently swells, and after sloping itself toward a green cone like a perfume box, gradually reddens, splitting and spreading out into a cup which encloses the yellow point that stands out of its center." He distinguishes twelve famous varieties recognized by his countrymen, roses that were grown in Greece, Asia Minor, Africa, and Spain. Among these is the Milesian rose with "its brilliant, fiery color, although it never has more than twelve petals." Pliny's red rose of Miletus was probably the species named *Rosa gallica* by Linnaeus.

Pliny laments the misuse of roses by the Romans, citing the case of a Roman banker who by authority of the Senate was led off to prison during the Second Punic War for wearing a chaplet of roses in the daytime on his porch overlooking the Forum. Chaplets, Pliny adds, are one of the least important uses of roses. The ancients used roses in innumerable ways, in decoctions, salves, even as preserves, or "as a coating for the delicacies of our tables." Pliny lists thirty-two remedies made from the rose.

In imperial Rome the rose ultimately became a symbol of voluptuousness and debauchery, although roses were also used at funerals. Brides and bridegrooms were crowned with roses, as were images of Venus, Bacchus, and Flora. Roses were scattered at wedding feasts, in the paths of victors, under chariot wheels, and on war vessels. They were used unsparingly at banquets: to garland guests and halls, to strew floors, and—even in winter—to float in Falernian wine. Romans washed with rose water, perfumed themselves with rose oils, ate rose puddings, and wore rose wreaths as antidotes to the intoxicating effects of wine.

Virgil and Horace both wrote about roses, Horace, on growing them in beds but against wearing them. In the *Georgics* Virgil refers to the first spring rose as well as to Paestum's rose gardens that bloomed twice a year *(biferique rosaria Paesti)*. *Rosa damascena* 'Bifera,' the Four Seasons or Autumn Damask, may have been this rose. Pliny's rose of Miletus is probably the *Rosa gallica 'Officinalis,'* well known as the Apothecary's Rose. These two ancient garden roses, as well as the wild *Rosa canina*, are among the old roses still grown today.

Full sun and ordinary garden soil.

The essential oil that gives the rose its perfume is found in the flowers of scented roses. Damask roses are used for the production of attar of roses and rose waters for perfumes; and petals of dark red roses, Rosa gallica *or modern garden hybrids, for medicines, syrups, and liqueurs. Rose hips, long in official pharmacological use for their refrigerant and astringent properties, are used now in medicine only incorporated in other drugs.*

ROSEMARY

ἡ λιβανοτίς

(libanotis)

Rosmarinus

*R*osemary in ancient Greece and Rome was the herb of memory, and a symbol of both love and death. Native to the Mediterranean region, rosemary thrives in arid soil along the coastlines, watered by the sea mists. Its name comes from the Latin *ros maris* or *rosmarinus,* dew of the sea, and Pliny remarks that it is never so richly flavored as when it grows near the shore. *Libanotis,* the name of the herb in Greek, actually means frankincense, and the scent of rosemary is likened to that of incense. One legend tells that the blood of the assassinated young priest, Libanus, fell on a rosemary plant. The rosemary took on the scent of incense in memory of his priestly vocation. Along with myrtle and mint, rosemary was customarily used in funeral rites in both Greece and Rome.

In Athens and Rome rosemary was placed in the hands of the dead. It was also worn by young couples at their marriage ceremonies. Both traditions were linked with remembrance and enduring affection. To sharpen their memories at examinations, Greek students twined sprigs of rosemary in their hair. Rosemary was also ever-present in wreaths and garlands for banquets and festivals, and it was an ingredient of magic spells and incantations. Placed under the pillow at night, it was thought to prevent nightmares. Rosemary was also one of the most frequently used green plants in Roman gardens, along with ivy, myrtle, bay, and oleander.

Theophrastus, Dioscorides, and Pliny all refer to *libanotis,* and two distinct medicinal herbs are given this name. The herb Theophrastus calls *libanotis* is not the rosemary we know. One of its forms has medicinally useful leaves and fruit—a fruit called *kakhry*— and a root that smells like frankincense. Dioscorides' herbal includes two varieties of *libanotis,* one that parallels that of Theophrastus and another that ''the Romans call *rosamarinus.*''

Dioscorides comments that those ''who weave garlands use it; its shoots are slender, about which the leaves, small, thick, somewhat long, flat; on the inside white but on the outside green, of a strong scent.'' For him, its chief medicinal virtue is as a sudorific, a substance that produces sweat: rosemary water is drunk before exercise, after which one bathes and then is splashed with wine.

Pliny in Book xix of his *Natural History* comments that ''*libanotis* grows in thin, powdery soil where there is heavy dew, it has a root like *olusatrum,* exactly like frankincense; when a year old it is extremely wholesome for the digestion. Some people call it by another name, *rosmarinum.*'' In Book xxiv Pliny mentions, probably repeating Theophrastus, that there are two kinds of rosemary: one is barren and the other has a stalk that produces a resinous seed called *cachrys*. This resinous capsule neutralized poisons and the venom of all creatures except snakes. Fresh rosemary root applied locally, he notes, heals wounds and hemorrhoids. Juice of the shrub and roots cures jaundice and sharpens eyesight. The seed given in drink helps chronic chest complaints and uterine trouble if taken with wine and pepper. An application clears freckles; it is used as a sudorific and also for sprains; with honey it is good for a cough.

References to the use of rosemary in cooking during antiquity are elusive, and perhaps like parsley its ritual uses prohibited more secular ones, at least in earlier times. Yet, its use by students and banqueters suggests broader applications. One can imagine an aromatic sprig of rosemary dipped in olive oil used to baste a fish or a fowl, much as is still done in Italy, and we know that the Apician cookbook prescribes a similar use of a fresh laurel twig to stir a sauce for roast suckling pig.

An evergreen, shrubby herb with linear, revolute leaves, dark green above and paler and glandular beneath. It has a pungently aromatic and somewhat camphoraceous odor. Flowers are small and vary from almost white to dark blue-purple. Much of the active volatile principle resides in their calyces.

Full sun to partial shade in light, rather dry soil, and a sheltered situation.

Contains some tannic acid, together with a resin, a bitter principle, and a volatile oil. Chief constituents of the oil are borneol, bornyl acetate and other esters, a special camphor similar to that of the myrtle, cineol, pinene, and camphene.

Tonic, astringent, diaphoretic, and stimulant.

Rosmarinus officinalis Linnaeus. *Labiatae.*

RUE

τὸ πήγανον

(pēganon)

Ruta

*R*ue in the ancient Mediterranean world was a powerful antidote for poisons and magic as well as the herb of sight. In later times the name *ruta* was said to derive from the Greek *rhyte,* relating to the drawing of an archer's bow, possibly because of rue's effectiveness in combating so many diseases. Hippocrates gave it a high place in his *materia medica* and it was one of the principal ingredients of the famous antidote for poison taken daily in small doses by King Mithridates, an early toxicologist, to immunize himself against poisoning. The meticulous historian Theopompus (born at Chios about 380 B.C.) was favored by Alexander the Great but later had to flee hostile regimes. In his fifty-eight-book history, *Philippica,* he reports that Clearchus, a tyrant of Pontus, was in the habit of forcing his subjects to take hemlock. As a result, those who were to be in his company always ate rue before leaving home.

The Greeks regarded rue as apotropaic for its power to alter conditions they thought were magically induced. Rue, for example, relieved indigestion brought on by eating before strangers, a discomfort that was attributed to magic. From earliest times rue was used to ward off contagion and to prevent attacks of fleas or other undesirable insects. Rue that was stolen from another garden was said to grow better.

Theophrastus, in classifying rue's characteristics and habits, notes that there is only one kind of rue cultivated and rue is exceptional among the pot-herbs because it dislikes fertilizer. Wild rue, he adds, has smaller, rougher leaves and stalks as well as a stronger, more pungent taste. Dioscorides attributes an unusually large number of remedies to rue, and like Theophrastus he reports that wild rue is sharper than cultivated and that the wild variety is unfit for food. The best for eating is grown near fig trees, probably a reference to the fact that rue prefers a sheltered position. He stresses the power of rue as an antidote for poisons: drunk in wine, the leaves taken by themselves, or with walnuts or figs. Mixed with polenta and applied to the eyes, it relieves pain. Rue juice warmed in a pomegranate rind makes good ear drops. He concludes with a saying that rue juice sprinkled on chicken keeps off the cats.

Pliny attributed eighty-four remedies to the use of rue! It is among the chief medicinal plants now, he says, and it was also highly regarded in the past. It should be sown when the west wind blows in spring and just after the autumn equinox; it hates cold, damp, and dung, and likes sunny, dry places. Honeyed wine with rue was given to the Roman public by Cornelius, Quintus Flaminius' colleague in the consulship, after the election (198 B.C.) Pliny underscores the power of rue as an antidote, as well as its effectiveness in improving eyesight. Dimness is dispelled by anointing the eyes with rue juice mixed

Ruta graveolens Linnaeus. *Rutaceae.*

with Attic honey, or even by touching the corners of the eyes with the pure juice. Pythagoras said wrongly, he continues, that it was injurious to the eyes, but Pliny points out that engravers and painters used rue as food with bread or cress to stay clearsighted. As a food, it is beneficial raw, boiled, or preserved. Pliny offers a final rue remedy: because eating rue slows down the generative process, it is prescribed for frequent amorous dreams.

Book x of the Apician cookbook includes a number of fish sauces that may be Roman versions of Greek recipes. Among them is *Ius diabotanon in pisce frixo,* a sauce of fines herbes for fish that offers the distinctive flavor and rich green color of rue:

> Clean and salt fish; dip in flour and fry in olive oil. Crush pepper, cumin, coriander seed, asafoetida, oregano, and rue; moisten with vinegar, date wine, must (grape juice), honey, and, oil *liquamen* (see page 29). Bring sauce to a boil and pour over fish. Sprinkle with additional pepper and serve.

Another sauce, *Aliter ius candidum in copadiis,* for appetizers or meat, is made with pepper, thyme, cumin, celery seed, fennel, rue (or mint), myrtle berries, raisins, and white wine sweetened with honey. It is simmered for about twenty minutes and should be stirred with a sprig of savory.

A hardy perennial. Leaves alternate, blue-green, musty-smelling, bi- or tri-pinnate on erect, stout, woody stems. Greenish-yellow flowers that resemble a cluster of stars are followed by red-brown seed pods that look hand-carved.

Full sun to partial shade in dry, stony, alkaline soil.

Volatile oil of rue is in the glands distributed over the whole plant and contains capric, pelargonic caprylic, and oenanthylic acids as well as a yellow crystalline body called rutin.

Strongly stimulating and anti-spasmodic.

Crocus sativus Linnaeus. *Iridaceae.*

SAFFRON CROCUS

ὁ κρόκος

(krokos)

Crocum

Saffron crocus was celebrated in Greek mythology and poetry. Homer praised "the saffron moon" and slept Zeus on a bed of saffron, lotus, and hyacinth blossoms. Gods and goddesses, nymphs and vestals dressed in saffron-colored garments. In the Homeric Hymn to Demeter the daughters of King Celeus "darted along the hollow path like well-fed deer and calves, lifting first the folds of their lovely gowns, and about their shoulders their hair shot out like crocus bloom." The herb was extravagantly admired for its perfume, its orange-gold hue, and its curative properties. Saffron water was sprinkled on theater benches, the floors of banquet halls were strewn with crocus leaves, and cushions stuffed with saffron blossoms. Its color had been a symbol of loyalty until it was usurped by the *hetairai,* the courtesans of Athens and Corinth.

Two quite different legends relate the mythological origin of the crocus. In one, the crocus sprang from the heat of Zeus and Hera disporting themselves on a grassy bank. In a more botanical story, a young man named Krokos died of unrequited love for the shepherdess Smilax and crocuses grew from his grave.

Hippocrates, Theophrastus, Theocritus, Lucretius, Virgil, Dioscorides, Pliny, Columella, and Martial also wrote about it, and the Greeks emerge as its strongest supporters in the ancient world. Saffron is the bright red stigma of *Crocus sativus,* cultivated from very early times by the Minoans who grew wealthy by exporting it all over the eastern Mediterranean world. Murals in the palace at Knossos on the island of Crete depict saffron harvesters at work. Long after the Minoan society had disappeared, saffron was almost as valuable as gold.

Aristotle wrote that saffron grew so abundantly on the Sicilian promontory of Pelorus that it was gathered there by the wagonload, although this seems unlikely and may be a reference to safflower, instead. Theophrastus was entranced by the saffron-colored countryside of Greece in the fourth century B.C., and he noted that the scent of saffron, which varied more than any other characteristic of the plant, was purest at Cyrene. In the *Georgics* Virgil entices the bees: "Let gardens sweet with saffron lure them on." A perfume in the Roman baths, saffron was sprinkled in the streets of the city when Nero entered Rome.

The saffron crocus is probably native to Asia Minor and Greece, but the ancients disputed the source of the best saffron. Theophrastus said Cyrene where it grew abundantly; Dioscorides said Corycia and after that Lydia and Olympus; the Romans preferred the saffron of Cilicia. Dioscorides describes a method for preparing a medicinal crocus oil which he terms *krokinon.* By pressing out the aromatic part of *krokinon,* a pastille called *krokomagna* was made, "sweet-smelling, somewhat resembling the savor of myrtle" with a "uretical, mollifying, concocting, and warming faculty."

Pliny is voluminous on the saffron crocus. He gives two tests for its purity: it crackles as though brittle and it stings the face and eyes. "It is nowhere used for chaplets," he comments, but powdered saffron in sweet wine is a "wonderful mixture to spray the theatre." The corms should be planted only during a few days at the setting of the Pleiades and gathered when green at the winter solstice. Saffron crocus likes to be trampled, he advises, and so treated it grows better. Saffron does not blend well with honey, or any sweet, but mixes easily with wine or water. It should be kept in a horn box. Medicinally, he reports, many remedies are made with saffron. It discourages intoxication, induces sleep, and is aphrodisiac. There are saffron ointments for eyes and ears, saffron compounds for gout and for procreating handsome children, and snails taken in food hasten delivery and also conception if combined with saffron.

Crocus sativus produces the flavoring, medicine, and dye used by the Greeks and Romans, and the plant that is still used today. The poisonous meadow saffron, *Colchicum autumnale,* was also known to the ancients: Dioscorides warns against it and calls it *kolchikon.* Excellent saffron grew wild in Italy, but the Romans preferred to buy the cultivated, prepared form from Greece. With the decline of Rome, saffron no longer was used as a flavoring. Later the Arabs brought it to Spain, where it is called *azafrán* from the Arabic *sahafaran* or the Persian *zahafaran.*

Crocus cartwrightianus is the wild Greek saffron common around Athens and the Cycladic islands. *Crocus sativus,* the fabled saffron crocus of the ancient world, is known only in cultivation. *C. cartwrightianus* is often considered a variant of and possibly a parent to the cultivated form. Both have the habit of remaining open at night and in bad weather, and both have brilliant scarlet stigmas that protrude between the petals. *C. sativus* produces narrow, grass-like leaves before the light purple flowers appear. Its rounded petals that open out flat in the sunshine resemble those of *C. cartwrightianus,* although the flowers of the wild variety are smaller and deeper in color. The crocus has a swollen underground stem, called a corm, which stores food during dormancy.

Expensive in antiquity, today it is the most costly of seasonings. An ounce of saffron powder requires the stigmas of more than 4,000 crocuses.

Well-pulverized soil, neither poor nor very hard clay.

Carminative, diaphoretic, emmenagogue.

Crocus sativus Linnaeus; *Iridaceae.*

SAGE

ὁ σφάκος

(sphakos)

Salvia

Sage has always been the herb of health, and it was one of the most important medicinal herbs in antiquity. Strabo, the first-century B.C. Greek geographer from Pontus, rated it first among the healthful herbs in his garden. Each year the ancient Greeks offered sage leaves to the hero Cadmus, who, according to legend, first discovered its healing virtues. Sage was also dedicated to Zeus and then later, in Rome, to Jupiter. Its generic name *Salvia* derives from the Latin *salvere,* to be in good health, because of its curative powers. It was included in the *materia medica* of Hippocrates, Dioscorides, and Galen and widely used by Roman physicians as a medicine for brain, stomach, and female organs.

Theophrastus differentiates between the cultivated, smooth-leafed *sphakos* and the rougher-leafed, wild *elelisphakos.* Dioscorides calls sage *elelisphakon* and describes it fully: "a rather tall shrub with many branches, four-square whitish stalks but leaves like malicotton yet longer, sharper, and thicker and hidden by hair, like outworn garments, exceedingly odoriferous, poisonous, with the seed at the top of the stalks like wild *horminum...* it grows in rough places." A decoction of its leaves and branches, he continues, is diuretic, emmenagogue, and will abort a dead fetus. Dioscorides also records a recipe for a medicinal sage wine: eight ounces of sage tied in a cloth are added to an amphora of grape must; after three months the liquid is strained into another amphora. He adds that sage is a wound herb, that it stops bleeding, and cleans wild ulcers. In white wine it cures pains of the spleen and dysentery. It also dyes the hair black. Pliny recommends it for some of these same uses, adding that it cures sting ray wounds and, when boiled down in wine, snake bite. "Our modern herbalists," he comments, "call this plant *elelisphacus* in Greek and *salvia* in Latin, a plant like mint, hoary and aromatic."

Perennial members of the mint family, of the 500 species of the genus *Salvia, S. officinalis, S. pomifera* L., and *S. triloba* L. fils, native to Greece and Italy, are the sages cited by classical authors as medicines and seasonings.

Sunny, sandy, alkaline soil.

Active principle a yellow or greenish-yellow volatile oil with a penetrating odor. Tannin and resin are also present in the leaves.

Stimulant, astringent, tonic, and carminative.

Salvia officinalis Linnaeus. *Labiatae.*

THYME

τὸ θύμον

(thymon)

Thymum

*T*hyme was a symbol of life energy to the ancient Greeks, of spirit and bravery. "To smell of thyme" was an expression of praise, and athletes anointed their chests with thyme oils before games to promote courage. The herb's generic name *Thymus,* thus, is thought by some to derive from the Greek *thymos* meaning courage. Others think it derives from the Greek word *thymiama* that refers to a substance burnt as incense, and an incense burner is called a *thymiaterion.* Thyme, crushed or as incense, was used for fumigating—producing fragrant smoke offerings—against evil and in sacrifice to the gods. Virgil refers to the use of thyme as a fumigant in his *Georgics* and Pliny informs us that burning thyme puts all venomous creatures to flight. The antiseptic properties of thyme also were fully recognized, as well as its many other medicinal values.

Blossoming thyme covered the hills of Hymettos as it still does today. Ovid's "purple hills of flowering Hymettos" refers to the wild thyme blossoms, and the honey made in this area then, as now, was considered the best in the world. So special was the honey of Mount Hymettos to the ancients that the idea of sweetness was equated with thyme. (Mount Hymettos thyme is *Thymus capitatus,* an upright subshrub which is sometimes given its own genus as *Coridothymus capitatus.*) Pliny remarks that Attic thyme was imported to Rome, but that it was difficult to grow in Italy partly because it required a sea breeze. All thyme, he adds, was once thought to require sea air; but there is a type that thrives now in the province of Gallia Narbonensis on stony plains.

The sweet smell of thyme also made it a popular component of the garlands beloved to the ancients. In a fragment by the Greek dramatist Eubolus, a garland seller recommends a wreath of thyme, "for who would forbear to kiss a girl who's wearing this?" Dionysius of Syracuse, famous for his lavish parties, strewed his palace with wild thyme before entertaining, partly because its pungent fragrance was considered aphrodisiac. These thymes were probably *Thymus vulgaris* or one of several species of creeping thymes native to the Mediterranean area.

About 300 B.C. Theophrastus noted that abundant thyme blossoms indicated a large harvest for the beekeeper. If rained upon, the flowers were injured, or even destroyed, but they thrived on a sea breeze. Cultivated forms of thyme are indistinguishable, he adds, but the wild kind—Attic thyme—is said to have more than one form. Of the mountain thymes one variety is like savory and very pungent, while the other is delicate and more fragrant. In his *Concerning Odors* Theophrastus also mentions the use of tufted thyme flowers in perfume.

Thyme appears in Hippocrates' *materia medica* as a healing herb, and in Dioscorides' herbal "*thymos (Thymus capitatus)* is known by all." Dioscorides recommends it for stomach

Thymus vulgaris Linnaeus. *Labiatae.*

complaints, asthma, worms, phlegm, and for dissolving blood clots. He also lists another thyme called *serpyllos* because it creeps, saying that it is the garden kind and is used for making garlands. A related variety he describes as wild and upright, growing on rocks, sweet-smelling, sharp-tasting, and better for medicinal uses than garden thyme. Pliny too catalogues several kinds of thyme. His *thymum,* or garden thyme, seems to be *Thymus vulgaris,* although he discusses Attic thyme as well as a wild creeping thyme that he calls *serpyllum,* used for medicines and garlands. Pliny's list contains twenty-eight disorders which thyme remedies, generally paralleling that of Dioscorides. Pliny adds that thyme taken in vinegar and honey cures hypochondria, mental aberrations, and melancholy. Epileptics are revived by its smell and should sleep on beds of soft thyme (probably *Thymus vulgaris*). Wild thyme drives snakes away.

Aristophanes praised a drink made from figs and thyme. Virgil was among those Romans who thought that thyme was an invigorating food, and we know that it was used as a salad green and to flavor cheeses. Apicius included thyme in *moretum,* a mixture variously described as a salad, a stew, and a cheese. It may have been a blend of herbs used as a bouquet garni. In the *Deipnosophists,* Athenaeus quotes a fragment from Callimachus who wrote: "I should like to satiate myself with thyme."

Identifying the thymes of the ancient Greeks and Romans is made more difficult by the use of the word *serpyllum* for creeping thymes by Varro, Pliny, Virgil, Dioscorides, and other classical writers. The *Thymus serpyllum* we know today is not native to Italy but rather to northern Europe. *T. serpyllum* is the name given by Linnaeus in the eighteenth century to a northern species of creeping thyme of which he was aware. Classical references to *serpyllum,* thus, are either to *Thymus vulgaris,* which does layer itself as a mature plant, or to one or more of the complex of small creeping thymes native to Italy, specifically, *T. glabrescens, T. longicaulis,* and *T. praecox.*

Thymus vulgaris is a semi-prostrate subshrub with a woody, fibrous root and numerous hard, branched stems. Small, linear, elliptical leaves are set in pairs. *Thymus capitatus* is a small upright shrub with vertical branches. It has narrower, linear leaves clearly arranged in two ranks that make a cross when seen from above.

Calcareous, light, dry, stony soil.

Chief constituents of oil of thyme are 20-25% of the phenols thymol and carvacrol. Cymene and pinene are also present as well as a little methone.

Antiseptic, antispasmodic, tonic, carminative.

GLOSSARY

apotropaic	A substance, gesture, or amulet that averts evil; anti-magic.
asafoetida	*Ferula foetida* Regel, *Umbelliferae;* commonly called Food of the Gods or Devil's Dung; the fetid, gummy oleoresin extracted from its roots used in antiquity as both medicine and seasoning.
benjamin	*Styrax benzoin* Dryand. *Styraceae,* or a related plant, which yields gum benzoin.
calyx, calyces	The whorl of leaves forming the outer covering of a flower bud.
carminative	A medicine that expels gas from the alimentary canal.
cultivar	In botany, a single clone which usually arises in cultivation and is propagated vegetatively.
decoction	An extract obtained by boiling.
demulcent	An application that softens, soothes, and reduces irritation.
diaphoretic	An agent that promotes perspiration; a sudorific.
drachma	An ancient Greek silver coin.
emmenagogue	A medicine that promotes menstruation.
emetic	A medicine that causes vomiting.
emollient	An application that softens or soothes.
erysipelas	A local febrile disease accompanied by intense inflammation of the skin.
hellebore	*Helleborus officinalis* Sibthorp, *Ranunculaceae;* the black hellebore used in antiquity as a powerful purge.
hemoptysis	Spitting of blood.
herbal	A book of names and descriptions of herbs; belonging to, consisting of, or pertaining to herbs.
herbal simple	A single plant or herb employed for medical purposes.
Linnaeus	(1707-78). Swedish botanist and taxonomist; founder of the binomial system of nomenclature and originator of modern scientific classification of plants and animals.
liquamen	A liquid seasoning made from fermented fish; often elaborated with herbs, vinegar, oil, or wine (see page 29).
lovage	*Levisticum officinale* Koch, *Umbelliferae;* an aromatic herb native to the Mediterranean area; used in antiquity as both food and medicine.
must	New wine; unfermented or partly fermented grape juice.
pinnatifid	A compound leaf with a series of leaflets arranged on either side of the leafstalk.
polenta	Boiled cornmeal, used as food or as a component of medicines.
pot-herbs	Herbs cultivated in kitchen gardens, i.e., herbs grown for boiling in the pot as decoctions, foods, or seasonings.
revolute	In botany, rolled backward, downward, or outward.
sesterce	A Roman coin; one-quarter of a denarius.
squill	*Urginea scilla* Steinheil *[Scilla maritima* L.*], Liliaceae;* a bulbous-rooted seashore plant widely used as a medicine in antiquity.
stigma	In flowering plants, that part of the pistil that receives the pollen in impregnation.
sudorific	An agent that promotes perspiration; a diaphoretic.
sumptuary	Pertaining to or regulating expenditure.
taxonomic	Plant classification according to natural relationships.
toxicologist	A person versed in the science of poisons.
trompe l'oeil	An artifice that fools the eye.
whorl	A set of leaves, flowers, or parts of the flower, springing from the stem at the same level and encircling it.

SELECTED BIBLIOGRAPHY

Abbe, Alfriede, *The Plants of Virgil's "Georgics"*, Ithaca: Cornell University, 1965.

André, Jacques, *L'alimentation et la cuisine à Rome*, Paris: Librairie C. Klincksieck, 1961.

Athenaeus, *The Deipnosophists* [Sophists at Dinner], trans. C.D. Yonge, 3 vols., London: Henry G. Bohn, 1954.

Bowles, Edward A., *Handbook of Crocus and Colchicum for Gardeners*, 2nd ed., Toronto: Van Nostrand, 1952.

Brothwell, Don and Patricia, *Food in Antiquity: A Survey of the Diet of Early Peoples*, London: Thames & Hudson, 1969.

Caldwell, Helen, *Ancient Poet's Guide to UCLA Gardens*, Los Angeles: Regents of the University of California, 1968.

Cato, Marcus Porcius, *On Agriculture*, and Marcus Terentius Varro, *On Agriculture*, Loeb Classical Library, trans. William D. Hooper, 1 vol., Cambridge: Harvard University, 1936.

Clair, Colin, *Of Herbs and Spices*, London and New York: Abelard-Schuman, 1961.

Donato, G., M.E. Branca, and A. Rallo, *Sostanze odorose del mondo classico*, Venice: CNRR, 1975.

Evans, Lesley C., "Roses of Ancient Rome," *The Rose Annual 1978*, St. Albans, England: Royal National Rose Society.

Flower, Barbara, and Elisabeth Rosenbaum, *The Roman Cookery Book: a critical translation of The Art of Cooking by Apicius for use in the study and the kitchen*, London: George G. Harrap, 1958.

Grieve, Maude, *A Modern Herbal: The Medicinal, Culinary, Cosmetic and Economic Properties, Cultivation, and Folk-Lore of Herbs, Grasses, Fungi, Shrubs, and Trees with all their Modern Scientific Uses*, 2 vols., New York: Dover, 1971.

Grimal, Pierre, *Les Jardins Romains*, 2nd ed., Paris: Presses Universitaires de France, 1969.

Hamilton, Edith, *Mythology*, New York: New American Library, 9th printing, 1965.

———————— *The Greek Way*, New York: New American Library, 7th printing, 1956.

———————— *The Roman Way*, New York: W.W. Norton, 3rd printing, 1965.

Hesiod, *The Works and Days and the Theogony*, trans. Richmond Lattimore, 1 vol., Ann Arbor: University of Michigan, 1959.

Hurst, Rona, "The Minoan Roses," *The Rose Annual 1967*, St. Albans, England: Royal National Rose Society.

Huxley, Anthony, and William Taylor, *Flowers of Greece: and the Aegean Islands*, London: Chatto & Windus, 1977.

Jashemski, Wilhelmina F., *The Gardens of Pompeii: Herculaneum and the Villas Destroyed by Vesuvius*, New Rochelle, New York: Caratzas Brothers, 1979.

Kerényi, C., *The Religion of the Greeks and Romans*, New York: Dutton, 1962.

Kitto, H.D.F., *The Greeks*, Middlesex and Baltimore: Pelican Books, 1972.

Kreig, Margaret B., *Green Medicine: The Search for Plants that Heal*, Chicago: Rand-McNally, 1964.

Ovid, *The Metamorphoses*, trans. and intro. Horace Gregory, New York: New American Library, 1960.

Pliny, *Natural History*, Loeb Classical Library, 10 vols., trans. H. Rackham, Cambridge: Harvard University, 1938.

Root, Waverley, *Food*, New York: Simon and Schuster, 1980.

Singer, Charles, "The Herbal in Antiquity," *Journal of Hellenistic Studies*, vol. 47, 1927.

Smith, Wesley D., *The Hippocratic Tradition*, Ithaca and London: Cornell University, 1979.

Tannahill, Reay, *Food in History*, New York: Stein and Day, 1973.

Theophrastus, *Enquiry into Plants*, Loeb Classical Library, 2 vols., trans. Arthur Hort, London: William Heinemann, 1916.

Thomas, Graham Stuart, *The Old Shrub Rose*, London: Phoenix House, 1956.

Thomson, William A. R., *Herbs that Heal*, New York: Scribner's, 1976.

Virgil, *Georgics*, trans. Smith Palmer Bovie, Chicago: University of Chicago, 1956.

Wasson, R. Gordon, Carl A.P. Ruck, and Albert Hoffman, *The Road to Eleusis: Unveiling the Secret of the Mysteries*, Ethno-mycological Studies No. 4, New York and London: Harcourt, Brace Jovanovich, 1978.

Wheelwright, Edith Gray, *The Physick Garden*, London: Jonathan Cape, 1934.

Ancient Roman Gardens, eds. Elisabeth B. MacDougall and Wilhelmina F. Jashemski, Dumbarton Oaks Colloquium of the History of Landscape Architecture VII, Washington, D.C.: Dumbarton Oaks, 1981.

Flora Europaea, ed. T.E. Tutin et al, 5 vols., Cambridge: Cambridge University, 1972.

Garden Lore of Ancient Athens, Princeton: American School of Classical Studies at Athens, 1963.

The Greek Herbal of Dioscorides, trans. John Goodyer, 1655, ed. Robert T. Gunther, New York: Hafner Publishing, 1959.

Hippocratic Writings, ed. with intro. by G.E.R. Lloyd, Hammondsworth and New York: Pelican Books, 1978.

The Homeric Hymns, trans. Charles Boer, Chicago: Swallow Press, 1970.

The Survival of Antiquity, Smith College Studies in History, Volume XLVIII, in honor of Phyllis Williams Lehmann, Northampton, Massachusetts: Smith College, 1980.